BUT ENOUGH ABOUT ME

GENDER AND CULTURE

CAROLYN G. HEILBRUN AND NANCY K. MILLER, EDITORS

GENDER AND CULTURE

A SERIES OF COLUMBIA UNIVERSITY PRESS

EDITED BY CAROLYN G. HEILBRUN AND NANCY K. MILLER

GENDER AND CULTURE READERS

But Enough About Me

WHY WE READ OTHER PEOPLE'S LIVES

Nancy K. Miller

COLUMBIA UNIVERSITY PRESS   NEW YORK

COLUMBIA UNIVERSITY PRESS
Publishers Since 1893
New York   Chichester, West Sussex

Copyright © 2002
Columbia University Press
All rights reserved

Library of Congress
Cataloging-in-Publication Data

Miller, Nancy K., 1941–
But enough about me :
why we read other people's lives /
Nancy K. Miller
p. cm. — (Gender and culture)
ISBN 0–231–12522–4 (acid-free paper)
ISBN 0–231–12523–2 (pbk. : acid-free paper)
1. Autobiography.
2. Women—Biography—History and criticism.
3. Aging—Psychological aspects.
4. Feminist literary criticism.
5. Miller, Nancy K., 1941–
I. Title. II. Series.
CT25 .M485   2002
305.4ʹ092—dc21   2002019241

Printed in the United States of America
Designed by Audrey Smith
c 10 9 8 7 6 5 4 3 2 1
p 10 9 8 7 6 5 4 3 2 1

For Victoria

CONTENTS

ILLUSTRATIONS

During the 1990s, after turning fifty, I found myself turning toward the past—reading memoirs nonstop and writing about them. I came to see my life as an unwitting but irresistible collaboration between other texts and other lives. Sometimes my identifications with the stories *not* about me (not even remotely) came to feel like a rediscovery of my own life and memories, like a haunting. In the same way, the hope expressed in the self-irony of my book's title is, of course, that *But Enough About Me*, the book that has emerged from my experience of reading other people's lives, will also make readers feel that the stories I tell bring back something of yours—your lives, your memories.

In *But Enough About Me* I tell three interlocking tales: how a girl who grew up in the 1950s became a feminist critic in the 1970s; how this unexpected development was shared with a generation of other literary girls in the academy; and how, in the course of an academic career, I (the girl) came to see myself as part of a wider narrative about women and aging. The stories appear in fragments that follow the familiar chronologies of an academic life.

For a long time I've measured my life by decades—in part, I think, because I was born with one, or almost. Given to retrospectives, I like to align my personal history with the times. For me the fifties were my coming of age; the sixties were my twenties, the seventies my thirties, the eighties my forties. At fifty I wanted to sort out the choices I had made (even if they didn't always seem like choices at the time), both intellectual and personal ones (like becoming a feminist)—and on the threshold of the new decade, the nineties, looking back, I wanted to revisit that story. Now, at the beginning of the twenty-first century, in reviewing my own life I've wanted to highlight the intersections of individual and collective turning points—from the decade of the decorous 1950s through the show-and-tell exhibitionism of the 1990s. And in that sense too the book is not only about me but about the uses (and abuses) of personal history in the making of cultural memory.

Autobiography is always most literally a curriculum vitae—the course of a life—but the slightly perverted model of selfhood as career narrative is a particular form of life writing that shapes many academic memoirs, including my own. Sometimes I think that without a c.v. I could never reconstruct my life. Having spent almost my entire life in school—first as a student, then as a teacher—I sometimes fear that my autobiography *is* my curriculum vitae, not to say my report card. But, even if it's a bright thread, that's not the only story I tell in this book.

The power of life writing in its various forms depends upon a tension between life and text that is never fully resolved. As Philip Roth quotes his alter ego, Zuckerman, in the epigraph to *The Facts: A Novelist's Autobiography*: "And as he spoke I was thinking, *the kind of stories that people turn life into, the kind of lives that people turn stories into.*" This ambiguous back and forth between lives and stories, between experience and history, has been crucial to the creation of feminism and central (for better or for worse) to the evolution of confessional culture in the nineties more generally. It's in that sense that *But Enough About Me* might be seen as part of a collective memoir—a group biography that chronicles the transformation of women's lives after the social and political upheaval of the 1960s.

How I lived those changes is the subject of the chapters entitled "Decades" and "Circa 1959." The installments of that story reflect a pleasure and an anxiety that seem permanently inter-twined. Both emotions come from having been part of something that actually happened—being present at the creation of a body of work called feminist criticism. A fifties' girl became a seventies' feminist. This is shorthand for how I gave up worrying about men and started worrying about my work. Not that I instantly gave up worrying about men. But if not for feminism—here comes the conversion narrative behind my autobiography—I would never have found either work I could do well, work that became a career, or a man I could actually live with.

If the book begins with a meditation about turning fifty and the sprawling landscape of personal culture in the nineties, it ends on the threshold of the next decade—which is to say, though I can barely bring myself to say it, that of my sixties. I did not welcome that decade of my own chronology with the sense of excitement and curiosity with which I approached (like the rest of the world) the new millennium. Stuck in a depressive turn-of-century miasma, I dreaded the year 2001, which was also the occasion of my fortieth college reunion. The chapter of this little melodrama, entitled "The Marks of Time," dwells on how, in the light of these particular turning points, the shape of women's lives takes on unexpected meaning both in relation to themselves (the mirror) and to other women. Contemplating women contemplating their faces and bodies at fifty and at sixty, I look for different (less depressing) ways to read the signs of change, as well as for styles of feminine resistance.

Last but in all ways not least, *But Enough About Me* is also organ-ized by a plot *not* about me. This is something like a back story about the nature of autobiography as a form and a practice. Explic-itly in the chapter really not about me, "Why Am I Not That Woman?" as well as in "But Enough About Me, What Do You Think of My Memoir?" I explore two propositions: the first, that the subjects of life writing (memoir, diary, essay, confession) are as much others as ourselves; the second, that reading the lives of other people with whom we do *not* identify has as much to tell us (if not more) about our lives as the lives with which we do. On the assumption that we read autobiographical writing in order to learn something about ourselves as well as about others, disidentification takes us as readers on a (sometimes circuitous, which is the whole point) journey back to ourselves. The tag "enough about me" owns up to the sin of self-involvement but also confesses the need for that of others.

What do my memories call up for you?

"My Grandfather's Cigarette Case," the epilogue to all this, is a fable of sorts about the limits of memory. From its beginnings in a cemetery, "My Grandfather's Cigarette Case" circles around the unsolved riddles, the silent ghosts of my family plot. In the end, though, like the rest of the book, what the epilogue reveals are the surprising pleasures of not really knowing the story you think reveals the most about you—and because of that strange ignorance, the chance of still having stories to tell.

ACKNOWLEDGMENTS

I wish to thank my editor Jennifer Crewe for her support of this project, her responsiveness as a reader, and the sureness of her critical judgment. I also wish to express my immense gratitude to Carolyn G. Heilbrun, Jane Opper, Jay Prosser, and Victoria Rosner, for reading the manuscript in its entirety—and as always to Sandy Petrey, title maven and severest critic. Lastly, I'm indebted to Susan Heath, manuscript editor, for her intelligence and tact, and Elizabeth Hollow for editorial generosity.

Portions of this book have appeared previously in somewhat different versions: "But Enough About Me, What Do You Think of My Memoir?" in *Yale Journal of Criticism* 13, no. 2 (2000): 421–436, © The Johns Hopkins University Press; "Decades" in *The South Atlantic Quarterly* 91, no. 1 (Winter 1992): 65–86, © Nancy K. Miller, 1992, *Wild Orchids and Trotsky*, ed. Mark Edmundson (New York: Penguin, 1993), © Nancy K. Miller, and *Changing Subjects: The Making of Feminist Literary Criticism*, ed. Gayle Greene and Coppélia Kahn (London and New York: Routledge, 1993); "Circa 1959" in *Feminism and Autobiography: Texts, Theories, Methods*, ed. Tess Cosslett, Celia Lury, and Penny Summerfield (London and New York: Routledge, 2000); "The Marks of Time" in *Figuring Age: Women, Bodies, Generations*, ed. Kathleen Woodward (Bloomington: Indiana

University Press, 1999); "Autobiography's Others" in *Sites* 2, no. 1, part 2 (Spring 1998): 127–139.

I gratefully acknowledge permission to reprint:

Lines from "To Waiting," W. S. Merwin, © 2001 by W. S. Merwin.

Lines from "Annus Mirabilis," in *Collected Poems* by Philip Larkin (London: Faber and Faber, 1990).

I am grateful to Terry Dennett for permission to publish photographs that appeared in Jo Spence's *Cultural Sniping: The Art of Transgression* (London and New York: Routledge, 1995). Photographs courtesy of the Jo Spence Archive.

BUT ENOUGH ABOUT ME

1

But Enough About Me,
What Do You Think of
My Memoir?

I

What were the nineties? The Clinton era will go down in history not just for the halcyon days of an endlessly touted national prosperity and the explosion of dot-com culture but also for a paroxysm of personal exposure: making the private public to a degree startling even in a climate of over-the-top self-revelation. If Clinton's performances stood the feminist dictum of the personal being the political on its head, the impulse of ask and tell was in no way unique—and not being shocked was, well, very nineties. The nineties also saw the spectacular rise of the memoir, which (along with biography) became the most popular (and symptomatic) literary genre of our contemporary culture.

In academia, going public as a private subject was equally in vogue as a kind of fin de siècle gasp of self-exploration with roots, arguably, in an earlier feminist critique of universal values. Like the memoir, personal criticism and other autobiographical acts (sometimes described by the neologism "autocritography") flourished in the 1990s, only to be diagnosed at one point by a disgruntled self-designated feminist critic as the "nouveau solipsism."[1] On the more positive side, a shrewd critic of shifting academic trends has recently recast the vogue of personal criticism as the "new belletrism"—a mode of writing keyed to a "reconfiguration of audience and audience expectations" (417).[2] But belletrism, of course, with its overtones of stylish self-indulgence is a dubious distinction for those who mourn the loss of literary standards, critical objectivity, and philosophical rigor. (There's an essay to be written about the use of French terms—nouveau solipsism, belletrism, not to mention memoir itself—to cast opprobrium upon what appears to be an American emotional style of self-reference.)

I want to move away, though, from the phenomenon of criticism produced for the academy to writing designed, like that of belletristic criticism, for the less specialized audience of memoir readers. But not without a parting shot (admittedly as a practitioner of nouveau solipsism), since both modes are at stake for me in this book. I'm going to suggest that like personal criticism, the genre of the memoir is not about terminal "moi-ism" (as it's been called) but, rather, a rendez-vous with others. Put another way, it takes two to perform an autobiographical act—in reading as in writing.

The relational tie binding self to other has historically shaped the narrative of most autobiographical experience, beginning with St. Augustine and Monica, whose death, we might say, engenders the *Confessions* (though a dead mother is not a prerequisite to life writing). Feminist literary critics and theorists have argued persuasively that this sense of relational identity has characterized women's lives in general and life writing in particular; this is largely true. Still, it's no less true that in postmodern culture the writing autobiographical subject—female or male—almost always requires a partner in crime—and often that partner is the reader.

This relational mode typically portrayed within autobiographical texts is also the model of relation that organizes the experience of reading autobiography itself. The bonds and desires that attract readers to the contemporary memoir have everything to do with attachment. What seems to connect memoir writers and their read-ers is a bond created through identifications and—just as impor-tantly—disidentifications. Although some degree of identification, conscious or unconscious, is typically present in reading prose nar-rative (fiction or nonfiction), memoir reading can't do without it. It's precisely the heightened process of identification that sends readers to the biography section (which is where you have to go to find autobiography) in such large numbers. And of course, the other side of this desire is the author's wish to be encountered in this way, found on that particular shelf. Writers of autobiography and readers of autobiography are codependent. Writing autobiog-raphy, like reading autobiography, can be addictive.[3]

II

How do you remember your life? How can you even tell it's your life, and not that of your tribe? In *The Woman Warrior*, her classic memoir about growing up Chinese American in postwar Califor-nia, Maxine Hong Kingston puts the problem this way:"when you try to understand what things in you are Chinese, how do you sep-arate what is peculiar to childhood, to poverty, insanities, one fam-ily, your mother who marked your growing with stories, from what is Chinese? What is Chinese tradition and what is the movies?"[4] How, I ask myself in translation, can I separate the story of my life from that of any nice Jewish girl who grew up middle-class in New York in the 1950s? For me, movies are like memoirs (and memoirs are like home movies). When I read the lives of others, I also see my childhood, my mother, the craziness of my family.[5]

Since the connections established between a reader's life and a writer's text are often more easily seen in the case of memoirs that emerge from the experience of a generation, I've chosen memoirs from a generation that almost overlaps with my own: Joyce John-son's *Minor Characters* and Hettie Jones's *How I Became Hettie Jones*.[6] Both tell a coming-of-age story that takes place in Manhattan dur-ing the 1950s when New York, especially Greenwich Village, was

3

home to an astonishing number of ambitious young people seduced by the same dream.

In her prizewinning 1983 memoir Joyce Johnson wittily relates the adventure of a rebellious, female adolescent who fell in with a group of writers who were about to become very famous. Here's a shorthand version of how Joyce met the Beats.

In 1951, after graduation from Hunter College High School, a competitive school for girls, Joyce, then Glassman, set out for her freshman year at Barnard College. She was not quite sixteen. Her parents lived around the corner from the Barnard Campus on 116th Street, and so she lived at home, not in a dorm, which cramped her sexual style. Avid for experience, Joyce scandalously escaped from parental control by moving out to live on her own without finishing her senior year. But here's the thing that made her more than just another female rebel without a cause. Fixed up on a blind date by Allen Ginsberg, a former Columbia student, Joyce met Jack Kerouac, another Columbia boy, and for a while became his girlfriend; Joyce was with Jack when *On the Road* was published in 1957. Joyce walked at midnight to the newsstand with Jack to read the review that brought him fame and put the word "Beat" into media currency. The subtitle on the cover of Johnson's memoir when it was republished in paperback in 1990 emphasizes that connection: *A Young Woman's Coming of Age in the Beat Generation*.

When I first read *Minor Characters* I had an eerie tingling of identification, of me too and what if. . . . Six years after Joyce headed for Barnard, another rebellious middle-class girl, me, followed those same steps and the same logic (though I was, I confess, already sixteen). I lived eleven blocks further south on Riverside Drive and lived miserably at home while at school. I too had gone to horrible Hunter College High School. Like Joyce I knew by the time I was a senior that what I wanted to learn was not to be found grubbing grades in our all-girls' school, and that "Real Life" as she named the universe of her desire was elsewhere. "Real Life," Johnson quips, was "not to be found in the streets around my house, or anywhere on the Upper West Side. . . . Real Life was Sexual" (31). This Real Life was the opposite of what my parents called the Real

World by way of discouraging any fantasies of sexual experience. This Real Life, which like Joyce's my parents strenuously inveighed against, sent the curious downtown in disguise on the subway of desire that takes you to the Village.

Now if I had only gone to Barnard six years earlier, would I have run into Jack Kerouac instead of my Columbia boyfriend? Hung out with Ginsberg and the Beats? Written a famous memoir? How much more exciting life might have been, if only. And sometimes you come close. You narrow the degrees of separation. (A friend of mine, who went to Barnard around the time that Joyce and her pals did, likes to tell a story about being introduced to Kerouac at the home of a Yale professor while she was in graduate school but turning down Jack's casual offer, without preliminaries, to "go upstairs.")

It's kind of like prescription drugs: she's the brand name, you're the generic. Still, am I so wrong to be seduced by the resemblance? Setting Jack aside, for the moment, I recognize myself fleetingly but intensely in Joyce's most important woman friend in the memoir, Elise Cowen, whose sad story closes the volume. Elise hooks up briefly with a sensitive young man, Keith Gibbs, a student of Lionel Trilling, a would-be poet with "the wisp of a little mustache" (265). Keith Gibbs! I scrawl in the margins. I knew him too! I dated his brother. (Lots of exclamation points on these pages.) Anyway, Keith found Elise appealing. "He came upstairs with her that night" (266), Johnson writes of the first meeting between the two on the Lower East Side.

I knew Keith Gibbs slightly because I hung out briefly with his younger brother, Tam. The Gibbs brothers were from California, which gave them an ineffable glamour in New York. Like Keith, Tam had a wispy mustache beneath his snub nose, which he used to stroke provocatively. Tam wore cowboy boots and at the Folksinging Club played folk music on the guitar while he sang and looked deeply into your eyes. One day, after an informal concert at the club, Tam offered to give me free guitar lessons—in his room. I wanted to play too, even if I couldn't sing. Folk music seemed irresistibly sexy in 1957, like disco decades later, only in reverse garb. You'd pull on your jeans—not yet a designer item but, rather, the mark of some small claim to rebellion—a pair of dirty sneakers, possibly torn in a couple of places, a black turtleneck—and head down to a concert at Carnegie Hall. Preferably at midnight. My parents vetoed the private lessons.

Anyway, Elise and Keith briefly live together in Berkeley, and in a letter Elise tells Joyce of their plans to go to Mexico, a favorite Beat destination. They never make the trip, and a few years later Elise kills herself in New York, jumping from the window of her parents' apartment. During one of the druggy downtown years before her suicide, she had typed Ginsberg's *Kaddish* for him. Elise ends up a character in both Joyce Johnson's memoir and in Allen Ginsberg's journal, where she gets added to his list of the dead. "Elise was a moment in Allen's life. In Elise's life," Johnson remarks sadly, "Allen was an eternity" (82). And remembers the doomed practice of girls loving the wrong man—even if he was an amazing poet.

"Alone / Weeping / I woke weeping / Alone / In black park of bed" (271). A friend of Elise found these lines in a notebook after her death. The dark misery of the lines seems familiar. While still in high school, I had composed a sequence of cinquains called "Reflections at Sixteen." One of them sounds remarkably like Elise's lament. "Sitting / In the waiting / Room of Life, I wonder: / Will love come in time to save me / From night?" (If publishing this isn't bravery, what is?) Like Emma Bovary who, when young, read many books that had set her yearning, holed up in the tiny maid's room of my parents' apartment, I too was desperately waiting for something to happen. I check out my scars, the traces of my own death wishes, but I'm also caught up in another kind of identification. All these girls draped in black, waiting. Looking back, I suddenly feel close to these girls dying from love, or wishing to; the frustration, or the madness of not knowing what to do with their ambition and anger.

Over and over again *Minor Characters* lures me into pathways back to my past life that I had consigned to oblivion and now find hard to resist. This also makes my own experience feel more meaningful: not "merely" personal but part of the bigger picture of cultural memory. For despite the unmistakably generational resemblances, this shared feeling is not simply the literal biographical hook of coincidence—hey I knew him too—that condenses the degrees of separation. Rather, this is the memory of the zeitgeist at work, the undertow of cultural memory that pulls your personal reminiscence into its domain. When you read a memoir that has already given a life something like yours a shape, the shape and ethos of a generation—in my case Manhattan, the 1950s, places where I went to school, Barnard, Columbia—it gets harder to hold onto your sense of self-possession; the boundaries of your past self may start to blur around the edges.

But paradoxically, this loss can produce a gain: you can seize what it is that escapes the grid. Another's text can give you back your life. Memoir reading works like a kind of interactive remembering—where the screen prompts the construction of memory itself.

For instance. In her narrative of a girl's apprenticeship to writing, which *Minor Characters* also is, Johnson revisits a creative writing seminar at Barnard with Professor X. As she describes him, X is a "middle-aged man, who no doubt wishes he were standing before a class at Harvard." "How many of you girls want to be writers," he asks in a "tone as dry as the crackers in the American cultural barrel" (84). All the hands go up, including some sporting engagement rings. It's 1953. "The air is thick," she writes, "with the uneasiness of the girl students." At the sight of this avowed nervous collective female ambition, Professor X hits his stride. How wrong they are. If they were going to be writers, they wouldn't have signed up for his class. They wouldn't even be in school. "You'd be hopping freight trains, riding through America" (85). The hands go down. You have to get going if you want to write the great American novel, hit the road like Jack, not sit home like a modern day Penelope—or Joyce.

Four years later at Barnard in freshman English I encountered Professor Y, who adopted a subtler style of discouragement. At the end of the year I went to see Professor Y. He had given me an A-for the last exercise of the year, a short story in which I don't lose my virginity. (The parents of middle-class girls exhorted us to pre-serve our virginity with an almost maniacal intensity.) I wanted to know how to become a writer (I had received honorable mention for a story in an *Atlantic Monthly* contest for high-school students that had given me hope). "Read the Russians and keep a diary," he replied with one of his famously ambiguous smiles. I already had started a diary; I spent the summer reading the Russians. Was "read the Russians and keep a diary" a way of saying it's not enough to have a sensibility, a sex life, and a wish to be a writer? The suspicion killed my ambition. I didn't take courses in creative writing. Instead I transferred my desire for self-expression to foreign languages. Not Joyce. Wanting to be the heroine of her life, and not just another Barnard girl sneaking around having sex behind her parents' back, Joyce moved out of her parents' house and into a room of her own. To write a novel? Perhaps first to have the experience—then to make some kind of new meaning of it on paper. "As a writer, I would live life to the hilt as my unacceptable self, just as Jack and Allen had done." She would describe "furnished rooms and sex" (156)—too boldly, she thought, for the domesticated pages of the *New Yorker*.

The real question was whether there was anything to become—and how.

In *How I Became Hettie Jones* we get an idea of what road a girl could take to becoming someone, a woman she herself might want to know—eventually. "Meet Hettie Cohen" (1). That's the first line of the memoir. Like Joyce Glassman, Hettie Cohen, another nice Jewish girl, enters college in 1951, though more radically leaving home to do so, and returns ready for a life in New York—a life with a job, yes, but also a question. "What should I do now," she asks, "What should I do now to make myself happen? What's next?" (27). Hettie was determined to escape the fifties plot scripted for talented girls.

In 1955 Herman Wouk, author of the Pulitzer prize-winning novel *The Caine Mutiny*, published another bestseller called *Marjorie Morningstar*, and *Time* magazine, who put him on its cover, applauded the values the novel celebrates: chastity before marriage, home, husband, and children. A nice Jewish girl, Marjorie Morgenstern, longs to become Marjorie Morningstar, the actress; after a fling with Mr. Wrong and a "career" in the theater, she ends up as Mrs. Milton Schwartz, wife and mother of four. From the Bronx to Central Park West to the wealthy suburb Mamaroneck, this route was not what Hettie Cohen had in mind. She was moving in the opposite direction, leaving suburban Long Island for the Village to do theater and, as she puts it, make herself "happen."

In 1957 the effects of Marjorie Morningstar's story were eponymously attached to that stairway to oblivion: the marriage plot. As Hettie remembers it, the lawyer she is dating already sees her fate writ large: "Don't kid yourself," he warns, "the Village is okay now, but you'll end up in Mamaroneck with Marjorie Morningstar, wait and see" (26). The girl with dreams to be on stage herself and the lawyer who rides a motorcycle are sitting in their café not far from the place where the movie version of the novel—starring Natalie Wood and Gene Kelly—had been filmed. What's your life and what's the movies? Sitting at Rienzi's, a popular coffee house in the Village, Hettie Jones is troubled by the prediction. "People had warned me, but no one had ever presumed to predict me. What did he know that I didn't?" (26). A close friend of Hettie from their days of shared struggle in the Village, Joyce reflects on the anecdote in her own memoir: "Ambitious young men of the fifties," she observes, "often evoked the wayward Jewish princess of . . . Wouk's bestseller" as a way of proving your desires "inauthentic," talking you out of them (226–27); it was as though they knew better than you ever could what you really wanted and could prove it (in this art they resembled the parents of the girls who took their own ambition just a little too seriously).

Rereading my diary, I discover that one evening that same year, after a concert at Town Hall, I sat at the same coffee house with a boy from Yale called Eddie, who wore a camel's hair coat; I express my doubts about Rienzi's, "a touristy place in the Village." "Lots of pseudos," I note with condescension, "but 'nice.'" By the following week, Eddie's fate was sealed. "I'm kind of disgusted with

Eddie. He thinks he's an authority on everything. Damn, I'd like to tell him a thing or two." And then the killer touch: "I'll never kiss him." My mother, however, adopting the line of *Seventeen* magazine, urged me to keep dating him: "It's good experience," she'd say.

I seem to be following Hettie around in her life, the way I did with Joyce. Soon Hettie's lawyer is history; she's fallen in love with the rising star poet, LeRoi Jones, and suddenly wants a baby. "I didn't think," she writes, looking back, "about how this decision might affect my own ambitions" (60). Even more than marriage, babies change your life. Not having them too. And it's here that my story splits off from Hettie Jones to pursue a completely different direction, even if I discover that a decade later we both shopped at the same store in the East Village. This is one of those little jumps of recognition that remind you of your own life and what matters in it. Jones describes a storefront on East Sixth Street where three sisters from Ohio known as "the Plendas" made and sewed clothing of their own design. Dresses, pants, tunics, all made of knitted fabrics that moved with your body. My own sister—by then a neighbor of theirs on Sixth Street—was friendly with the Plendas and took me shopping there at the end of the sixties when I was back from my expatriate incarnation in Paris and starting my life over in graduate school. I loved their dresses, which had a way of skimming, almost skipping over your hips so that you could imagine yourself thin. One with a low scoopneck in black that I wore to a New Year's Eve party, feeling quite daring. And an austere dark green one with long sleeves that I wore to a lecture by Julia Kristeva. Whenever I wore it, I felt pencil thin—and self-possessed. You might think knit dresses a pretty tenuous thread for holding separate lives together in memory, crafted in the pages of other people's books. It is and it isn't.

The path of identification provides one of the major byways along which interactive remembering moves. You follow the threads that take you back, even if *then* there was no story, just the loose threads you see now woven into a readable fabric, material for another story: your own. Of course I've stacked the deck here by taking examples from the old neighborhood; it would have been more surprising had I found *no* connections to someone who went to the same schools I did, hung out in the same bars, crossed the same streets. But as we've just seen, too, I part company with Hettie when Cohen becomes Jones and a mother. And once again in retrospect my life has another kind of clarity: I didn't do that particular fifties thing; I went to Paris instead. In other words, disidentification turns out to be as important in the self-reconstructive effect of memoir reading as identification.

I've been emphasizing the ways in which autobiographical identification (and alternately, the splitting off of disidentification) passes through the proximity of shared experience; how when I read the memoirs of women whose lives were marked by the cultural template of the 1950s, I feel that the book has been written for me; just as Maxine Hong Kingston specifically addresses the Chinese Americans like herself whom she imagines reading *The Woman Warrior*. In fact, the question from the memoir with which I began is directed to the readers with whom the writer shares an ethnic legacy: "Chinese-Americans," she asks, "when you try to understand what things in you are Chinese," how do you know how you became who you are, what's you and what's the movies? But as we know, the audience for *The Woman Warrior* has readers across the globe who do not share in this cultural memory, this social history. Yet that difference in no way prevents them from taking an intense pleasure in the pages of this book.

So what happens when beyond even disidentification there seem to be no commonalities between your life as a reader and the writer's, when it's another zeitgeist entirely? What have you to do with a woman who had an affair with her father, a man who was a sexual addict, fill in the blanks with the person most unlike you that you can imagine. If the task of memoir is to pull away from the face you see in your mirror to contemplate a face that doesn't look like yours, what does it take to make an intimate connection? Put another way, can we respond only to memoirs written by our twin, as though we had been separated at birth?

Paradoxically, identification can also mean the desire to rediscover yourself across the body or under the skin of *other* selves, people who are nothing—seem nothing—like yourself, to time travel, to get away, to take a much needed vacation from . . . you (whoever that is).[7] Finding losing, losing finding. Who's who? But whatever the modality, the experience passes through acts of memory—the author's and yours, and through the passage between the two. In the back and forth between what's on the page and in your head, your "you" becomes text.

Like the passion for biography, the memoir craze feeds the hunger for a different, or at least more interesting, life through literature—even if the memoirs describe a life, like those of the biographies, plagued by suffering, illness, obsession, or madness. But with this twist: however hellish the lives, told in memoirs they give you just what your unrecorded history lacks (and that the novel used to offer): a narrative through which to make sense of your own past.

Why do so many people write and read memoirs today? It's the well-worn culture of "me," given an expansive new currency by the infamous baby boomers who can think of nothing else; it's the desire for story killed by postmodern fiction; it's the only literary form that appears to give access to the truth; it's a democratic form, giving voice to minority experience in an antielite decade; it's a desire to assert agency and subjectivity after several decades of insisting loudly on the fragmentation of identity and the death of the author. It's voyeurism for a declining, imperial narcissism. It's the market.

Difficult to think of a modern genre that has come in for the kind of rhetorical abuse that memoir seems to inspire. I'm not alone in thinking that the predominance of women writing memoirs may also have something to do with the genre's disrepute.[8] The other genre whose project, like that of the memoir, is attacked at the roots, is the eighteenth-century novel (also associated with women); like the memoir, the very grounds of the novel's existence are put into question from the start: Should readers believe that the letters put before them are true? In the case of memoir, it's the reviewers, who like the poeticians and censors of another era, police the arts. They seem to hate the form from its foundations, decrying its necessary component—the self. A diatribe published in *The Nation* declares war: "The memoir trend is not just a publishing ruse to get more people to buy more books. It's an intellectual fraud, a cultural fraud, a fraud perpetrated by us, in the end, upon ourselves and our past."[9] Flaying practitioners of the genre who privatize both history and memory, the journalist ends with his definition of what makes memoir a genre with a legitimate right to exist: "We arrive at a curious, unexpected truth: that the purely personal is not the stuff of the memoir but its enemy. Once this is understood, it becomes clear that the memoir does not have to be a symptom of our cultural decline, or our withdrawal, or our fading ability to imagine and create and then give form to our creations.... The trick is to embrace history, not oneself" (33). But as I hope you've seen, on my reading, the work of memory can't help being historical.

What's wrong with embracing oneself? In seventeenth-century France, Pascal famously diagnosed the matter in his analysis of human misery: "The self is hateful." ("Le *moi* est haïssable." Here we go again with more bad news from the French.) Why? because, Pascal says, "it is unjust in itself, to the extent that it makes itself the center of all."[10] This founding injustice is not a correctable flaw, however, because the delusion that the self matters above all is a symptom of what happens when man lives without God. It may seem far-fetched to reach back to seventeenth-century religious debates to make this point, but the utter conviction of the inherent inadequacy of the self—that entity that says "I" believing in the importance of his reality—that emerges from Pascal's credo, comes close to the almost religious fervor that underlies contemporary attacks on the literature of the self.

Does memoir really give narcissism a bad name? Or should we take it more seriously?

Here's my idea. One of the meanings of the word "memoir" is memorandum. And this meaning surfaces in another French expression that has passed into English: the aide-mémoire. Something that helps memory. I want to propose the notion of memoir as prosthesis—an aid to memory. What helps you remember. In this sense what memoirs do is support you in the act of remembering. The memoir boom, then, should be understood not as a proliferation of self-serving representations of individualistic memory but as an aid or a spur to keep cultural memory alive.[11]

We are witnessing a very powerful anxiety about memory, about remembering, very particular to our time: about gathering the testimony of the last living survivors of the Holocaust. In *Testimony* analyst Dori Laub makes a provocative claim, suggesting that the so-called culture of narcissism (famously diagnosed by Christopher Lasch in 1978) may be understood as a "historical diversion, a trivialization . . . a psychological denial of the depth and the subversive power of the Holocaust experience" (74).[12] We may be witnessing a kind of unconscious fear of erasure. Seen in this light, memoir is the record of an experience in search of a community, of a collective framework in which to protect the fragility of singularity in a postmodern world. Maybe it's not so surprising that we seem to need memoirs now, at a moment when a large segment of a booming aging population is literally stricken with Alzheimer's and when we are experiencing a kind of metaphorical Alzheimer's about, as former President Reagan put it, where the "rest of us" is, a kind of American anxiety about the end of a certain idea about life.

Memoir is the most generous of modern genres. Indeed, the point of memoir—when it succeeds—is to keep alive the notion that experience can take the form of art and that remembering is a guide to living. Toward the end of Stendhal's novel about self-transformation, *The Red and the Black*, Julien Sorel, the young hero, surveys the astonishing distance he has traveled and reflects upon his brilliant career. "My novel has ended," he exclaims almost sadly (though its final chapter was to surprise him). What is life beyond the novel, even, as Julien adds, one for which he deserves, he feels, "all the credit"?[13] At the beginning of the twenty-first century in American culture, looking to novels as a way of rereading your life sounds anachronistic (even mid-century, Hettie felt that way about the plot of *Marjorie Morningstar*).[14] In the nineties the novel got parceled out into movies, sitcoms, and most of all, memoirs. If like Julien Sorel my novel is over, my memoir isn't. I'm still looking for a way to have my life turn out better on paper, though not perhaps in reality. If you can't change the history of past events, you can supply a different interpretation, perhaps more interesting, to its outcome thus far. Thanks to other people's memoirs, you can time travel to a former self, though there are no guarantees you will like what you find—not least that person whose past you so intimately share. On the contrary, you may find "only yourself," as W. S Merwin writes in "To Waiting":

> with whom as you
> recall you were
> never happy
> to be left alone for long

III

When Diane di Prima published her long-announced memoir, *Recollections of My Life as a Woman: The New York Years* in 2001, I was curious to see what the sequel to her 1969 *Memoirs of a Beatnik* (also a story about the New York years) would offer.[15] A published poet, di Prima was the sole woman writer to gain recognition among the Beats. What did that era mean for women with artistic aspirations in light of Kerouac's remark that the Beats were just a "bunch of guys" who "were out trying to get laid"?[16] Di Prima's girl version of that story recounts sexual performances that show how easily (at least in fantasy) she matched the guys in bed (in fact, di Prima sounds more like a female Mailer than Kerouac, who is never long on detail). In *Memoirs of a Beatnik* di Prima fictionalized her sex life as an urban odyssey (migrating between apartments) in 1950s Manhattan. The book was commissioned, its author tells us in the afterword, by Maurice Girodias, Henry Miller's French publisher, who kept sending the drafts back scribbled over with the demand "MORE SEX" (137), with which the author seems to have complied. The crowning scene of Diane's coming-of-age story describes an orgy with Ginsberg and Kerouac (Diane gladly winds up with Jack, though more entertained by his antics than satisfied by his moves), already on their way as writers to the place they occupy today in the American cultural marketplace. *Memoirs of a Beatnik* ends soon after the orgy, with Diane discovering that she is pregnant (not, however, by Kerouac).

Would *Recollections of a Woman* mean still more sex? the birth of her baby? The memoir begins, as conventional autobiographies do, in childhood—di Prima's Italian American family in Brooklyn, the girl's passions and aspirations. I was curious, as I've said, but not because I anticipated the effects of identification like those produced by *Minor Characters* or *How I Became Hettie Jones*. In part I didn't expect a memory prompt because, unlike Glassman, Cohen, and me, di Prima wasn't Jewish (*the* defining category when I was growing up). I didn't expect to find connections to my middle-class nice Jewish girl life. But *Recollections* surprised me. Like Joyce Glassman (whose classmate she was) and me, di Prima attended Hunter College High School (which I didn't know when I read *Memoirs of a Beatnik*), and Hunter was an experience that marks a girl for life. (In fact, I had read about her in Hunter's *AlumNotes*. It's hard to picture beatnik di Prima sending in items for the school newsletter, and yet, there she is, hoping to attend her fiftieth reunion in 2001—and pitching her books.)

What happens, I wondered earlier, when you read the memoir of someone not like you, whose life took another, radically different path, but with whom you overlapped in time and space (like my shopping with Hettie Jones). Someone with whom on the face of it you have nothing in common, or in this case, nothing in common but a high school.

Even as a fantasy life, *Memoirs of a Beatnik* is daunting. What fifties girl could imagine, not to say live those scenes? The autobiographical "I" of *Recollections* is daunting in other ways, even if the procreation narrative has replaced the sequences of multiple orgasm—and partners.

From the morning I woke with the desire for a baby, till the point when I knew for certain I wanted no more children [she was to have five], I was at the mercy of this thing. This way of seeing. I was no longer simply with a man for himself, but for what kind of children he might make. And whether he'd leave me alone to raise them as I wished. This point of view intensified whenever my body demanded another child. But it was continuous, and never far in the background. (160)

Although I quite remember playing with my dollhouse and conjuring up five imaginary children (even their names), and although at a few crisis points in my life thought I wanted to have a (one) child, my desire to reproduce never reached this level of compulsion, not to say realization (we clearly belong at opposite ends of the fertility scale). Most of all, what I experienced was never quite a bodily desire; it was more like an idea.

The second child is a baby that di Prima has with (well, by) LeRoi Jones; the second pregnancy after an abortion that he had insisted on. The baby she wants will have Jones as its father, despite the fact that he is married to her good friend Hettie, who had also decided earlier in the story that she wanted a baby with Roi (as he was known to intimates in those days). In her memoir Hettie remembers how she got her wish: "With utmost ease I became careless about what I called my rubber-baby-buggy-bumper. . . . Stifling giggles at the cling of nylon tricot sheets, we fell into the hole in the middle of the unfamiliar bed and made a baby" (60–61). If her parents wanted her to abort, Roi didn't: "I guess we'll have to get married, then" (61).

Di Prima was on a different track. To justify the betrayal of a friend, she portrays herself as being driven by a higher necessity according to whose logic she was entitled to this child: that this "was my right . . . simply follow my Will, wherever it now led me" (267). Despite Roi's marked lack of enthusiasm—"If you really loved me, . . . you'd have an abortion" (268)—di Prima is determined to have the baby she willed into existence. "Roi was universally pitied," she admits (269). Friends thought Diane should have an abortion "and said so, Hettie Jones among them" (274). Hettie Jones doesn't include that opinion in her narrative, though she does note the affair and its aftermath. "So I wasn't surprised to learn that he and Diane di Prima were lovers—but the first affair cuts the cake, nothing else is ever as sharp." Reconstructing the moment of betrayal, Hettie shows remarkable generosity—"Diane was everything I wasn't"—and admires her freedom: "I never knew how she lived. . . . But Diane's life was her lit" (98). Seeing her old friend with the new baby "buggy to buggy" strains Hettie's tolerance: "I looked at the dark brow, the familiar features of Diane's baby. It was hard—*hard*—for me to admit she existed" (190). So was it for Roi.

However many babies, they never seemed to interfere with Diane's writing; while Hettie's poems struggled to be born, di Prima recasts her life as romantic literature. Of her relation to Roi: "I saw us as eternal and archetypal lovers. Mythmaking. At least as significant as Mary and Shelley. Outside the law, like Tristan and Isolde" (225). The love, death, high-art model coexists with a more prosaic fifties' girl mantra: "Make love, make coffee." Both streams come together in the glories of prefeminist womanhood: "*To be available*, a woman's art I saw as a discipline, a spiritual path. To be available, but stay on course somehow. Self-defined in the midst of it all: my life, my life" (226). When di Prima looks back over her years with Roi, she is overcome with admiration for her younger self, her exceptionality: there were no "women writers who were *artists* first, who held to their work as to their very souls" (223). (Not Hettie. Her work would be delayed: "there's an old kitchen way to say what we did," she writes about female casualties of the era, "you bury your talent in a napkin" [130]).

Despite my profound sense that the music of my own story departed radically in tone and line from di Prima's arias, I confess that I kept reading, fascinated by the unfettered display of self-aggrandizement on the part of someone I shared a school song with. "Reaching back today," di Prima writes in one of the rarer moments of meditation about the past, about reconnecting with the girl she was, "my flesh that of a woman of sixty, I try to remember, to reconstruct the feeling. What I do remember are the words in my mind: That if I didn't have a baby I was going to get sick. . . . Years later I would come to know that the body has a vegetable mind, like a plant. It has its own agenda and intent, separate from the mind, the heart, the Will" (156). Between her Will and her body's mind, nothing stands in the way of di Prima's ascent. I don't think my body ever had a mind, not to say an agenda. And I can't help feeling that all this is a giant rationalization for wanting Roi. (What did these women see in him, I keep wondering. But of course what girl wanted a nice guy.)

So the power of my disidentification comes not just from the fact that unlike the Jewish girls Glassman and Cohen, di Prima grew up the daughter of an Italian and Catholic family in Brooklyn. What makes di Prima at times seem to have descended from another galaxy rather than another borough is more the combination of Beatness (that turns New Age) and this reproductive compulsion. Di Prima ends her story on the West coast, meditating, writing—and having "founded a Magick school with friends" (424). Put it this way: even if I believed in something called magic, I would never spell it with a "k."

Everything that makes us different, that makes me say—no, not my story at all—is exactly what makes the memoir valuable to my own history. Di Prima's grandiosity reminds me how little I wanted a child (however much I've come to regret that) and how timid I was, even in my own mind, for so long about what I might have wanted. Reading di Prima reminds me of the girl I did not like being—the girl I was at Hunter. The part of my story I would prefer not to tell. I don't especially enjoy being reminded about her but I can't deny her either. Disidentification like identification comes with a price.

Contrary to its critics' views, memoir reading is an excellent antidote to narcissism and nostalgia.

Separated by a six-year interval, di Prima and I nonetheless had some of the same teachers, some of the same passions. Mrs. Lilienfeld, but di Prima has her first name, Ruth, and a piece of her life history: she "later went to Japan to study Zen." We both see our biology teacher seated in the place she occupied in the science classroom: "a small woman on a high stool" (73). In hygiene (a required course), Mrs. Lilienfeld, a tiny woman (petite). The shape of her beautifully sculptured head was accentuated by a pixie haircut. Mrs. Lilienfeld believed there should be no fake feminine modesty about sexuality or body parts. With utter serenity, she would make a huge class of giggly schoolgirls repeat after her "pen-is," "va-gi-na," slowly accentuating each syllable. Was that all we needed to know? I doubt that many of us at fifteen wanted to know much more. A classmate remembers that Mrs. Lilienfeld authorized us in certain circumstances not to wear underpants in the summer. She also instructed us never to sit with crossed legs because we would get varicose veins; she certainly turned out right about that in my case, though naturally I scoffed at the warning.

"Miriam Burstein, beautiful as her name" (73). (I can't help feeling that you'd have to have been an Italian girl to find beauty in that name.) In the yearbook, there's a picture of Miss Burstein (a teacher also evoked in Audre Lorde's memoir) with the members of the English department, smiling somewhat ironically, not wearing the horn-rimmed glasses I remember.[17] Even seated, Miss Burstein seems large. Looming, is how I remember her, standing, maybe leaning on the desk, so that her shoes—whatever came before "earth shoes"—are visible. Even more than her voice, I remember mainly the manner of speaking—of detached, almost smirky smartness (a Hunter trademark) that shaped her mouth, curled her lips when she passed judgment. But what did we read with Miss Burstein? I cannot remember. Di Prima attributes finding Keats—her inspiration for her ideas about poetry, about becoming a poet—in her class. "I came to Keats by way of Somerset Maugham, 'hack novelist' as Miriam Burstein called him in an English class. Maugham had quoted Keats: 'Beauty is truth, truth beauty'—was it in *Razor's Edge?*" (77). I liked Somerset Maugham too, especially *Of Human Bondage*. Would anyone confess to *Marjorie Morningstar?* Such were the lessons of Hunter—

what to eschew, hack novels by hack novelists, along with New York accents (dentalization, glottal stops) and bad posture.

Even as a freshman at Barnard, I had problems with literary taste. One of our first assignments, designed to teach us how to recognize great writing, used *The Poet's Craft*. In "Poems for Appreciation," two unidentified poems dealing with similar themes are compared and contrasted. Consider, Professor Y commanded, these two about the discovery of a new world (Columbus versus Cortez). I do not pick Keats's "On First Looking into Chapman's Homer." There is a terrible silence as Professor Y looks around the room with a mournful sigh.

Latin. Di Prima and I for once are in the same register of intensity, if not exactly speaking the same language. "French was okay with me [me too, though I was to love it later]. But it was Latin I was in love with. In spite of my ancient, crumbling, old-fashioned teacher. Structure and fluidity at once, like biology and physics coming together. And quirky surprises. I didn't know to call it linguistics. Light of the mind" (74). How could she have forgotten Dr. Corrigan's name? Dr. Corrigan spoke with what I imagined to be a Boston accent. Unmarried (I assumed) and (hence?) rigid, every cliché seems apt in a portrait of Dr. Corrigan: steely blue eyes, ramrod straight posture, white hair (read: old). Notably, Dr. Corrigan was the only teacher to use Delaney cards (have I invented them?). Slotted into columns of slits in a special notebook that lay open on her desk, the cards recorded every aspect of student performance. Looking at no one in particular, Dr. Corrigan would pick her victim, slide her card out of its pocket, call on her to read and translate. Never even the flicker of a warning. When it came to translating, I would know I was translating individual words correctly but, terrified as I was, I had no idea whether I was making sense as I went along attaching one word to another. But I got wonderful grades—the highest in any of my subjects (somewhere I have a Latin prize)—and there was no fooling Dr. Corrigan, so I must have been getting it right (did she even have a first name? suddenly I think: Lillian). My Latin is a pale trace of knowledge. (When I took the Latin exam in graduate school I had the luck of being assigned a passage from *The Aeneid*—a work that I could still remember translating in Dr. Corrigan's class, long after the actual words had faded.)

I've always found it strange that I retrieve names and scenes with great accuracy when whole chunks of information, people, events are missing, beyond my conscious grasp. Reaching back at sixty, despite my research I cannot get back into my fifteen-year-old's body. The girl has become archival—and I her archivist. Reading the memoirs of others is a goad to memory and at the same time the proof that memory is not enough, nor is research on a past self finally more than a prosthesis. If there is a lesson in the memoir genre, it's that all we have are flashes. Precious as they are, these flashes only take on meaning within a story—but a story of our willing (yes—that Will). They are more like a snapshot than a movie. And more—I have to admit—like fiction than history.

So back to di Prima. If our schoolroom memories overlap at places on our respective graphs, they necessarily add up differently in our memoirs. Which is just my point. It is not memory alone I'm after but the shape through which memory enters narrative. However generational memory may be, however dependent on a generation's values and social arrangements, each story has its singular contours: di Prima, like Audre Lorde, belonged to a group of self-defined misfits at Hunter called the "Branded." I'm not sure I would have recognized a group to belong to.

Except for those three teachers, little else about our Hunter years matched up. Just as siblings rarely have the same parents, schoolmates rarely attend the same school. For me school was from the beginning a scene of unrelenting anxiety about doing well on the one hand, about being excluded on the other. At Hunter the details of competition were refined. Grades were posted every quarter and your average calculated to two decimal points. There was your name, your grade, your quartile, and your place in the class. Hunter had its silly traditions—its all-girls-school rituals— but it was not a sentimental place and no one was spared; Hunter was not about feelings. It was not enough to be good at what you were good at; you had to be good at everything. Di Prima describes

Hunter as a place where she found herself, a place where it was "safe" for the first time to be incredibly smart. Hunter was, perhaps, more exciting for girls whose parents were not college-educated, closer to an immigrant generation than I was, and for whom Hunter was a path to a world that had seemed remote. Coming from a professional, middle-middle-class home, with parents who had gone to college (my mother had been a French major at Hunter College), Hunter was for me almost predictable in its values and style. Hunter was not different from my home; it was its evil twin, where every doubt I had about myself was publicly exposed. What my parents thought, my teachers graded.

But maybe the problem was finally not about Hunter but about me.

Di Prima is getting me down. I want to pose some resistance to the persona *her* persona brings out in me. I want to find a place to retrieve a countermemory of accomplishment. Occasionally the difference between di Prima in her memoir and me in mine is a matter of scale—and the scale tips in my favor. "At home," di Prima writes, "it would be 'Who do you think you are—Sarah Bernhardt'? whenever I 'got dramatic' as my parents put it—took myself seriously in any way" (76). The histrionic was frowned upon. My parents would have nodded knowingly at the evaluation of my emotional style by an English teacher at Hunter: "Excellent work. Inclined to dramatics in her emotional behavior."

There was one place where dramatics were encouraged and made another kind of sense. Dance. Modern dance was the thing in the 1950s. To look like a dancer was to have the look. I knew I would never be a dancer; I knew I didn't have the body or the talent; but I wasn't terrible either, and I had the requisite intensity. My mother had dragged me to classes at the YMHA from an early age, and when I was fifteen I took a summer course at the Martha Graham studio. Finally one thing I could do that di Prima couldn't (not to be competitive) was "contract and release." Di Prima could not make her spine curve (a physical problem identified only later in life) to perform the basic movement of the Graham body grammar: "contract and release" (151). I was great at contract and release.

Martha Graham, exactly like the photographs, at one with her image, would stride into the class, looking like Medea. Majestic. One wanted to please—Graham or her teachers. Even being wrong was worth it to be rewarded with her attention. Once she slapped me with the back of her hand across the thighs, commanding me to expand my turnout.

My most "dramatic" memory belongs to crossing the floor. We would walk on a diagonal making a gesture of pointing (dramatically) to the corner we were facing. The success or failure of the gesture was tied to the spirit of the arm's arc, the energy as the arm unfolded, rather than its actual reach. Graham would interrupt the student halfway across the floor if the feeling in her gesture was wrong—timid or overly graceful, balletic. Graham was looking for a kind of force (contract and release itself was in her view the body's breath put into motion). The interruptions were the high point of the class, for it was here that the essence of the instruction was delivered. Graham explained that in Hebrew the word for sin also meant to miss the mark, not hit the target. The only sin, she said, was not giving oneself over to the aim of the gesture: to fail to salute the imaginary person standing in the corner toward whom your body was moving. Maybe Graham was right for life off the floor as well.

IV

Johnson concludes *Minor Characters* with a double image: the first of herself, the girl, at twenty-two dressed entirely in black "like Masha in *The Seagull*—black stockings, black skirt, black sweater— but unlike Masha, she's not in mourning for her life." She regrets nothing about those years of excitement and passion, especially not her "seat at the table in the exact center of the universe," as she puts it, "the only place in America that's alive" (276). She does not even regret, she says, the fact that women had no voice at that table then, as long as she speaks of it now: Elise's poetry in homage to Pound, "and the poems Hettie kept mute in boxes for too many years."

This act of breaking the silence is not meant as the final word, and the paper journey has to end somewhere. The last lines of the book offer an image of memory working itself out temporally, in a musical metaphor: "I'm a forty-seven-year-old woman with a permanent sense of impermanence. If time were like a passage of music, you could keep going back to it till you got it right" (277). Of course time isn't a passage of music and there's no way to get it completely right. It's no wonder that just as you might think you've gotten to the end you discover that every memory trunk has fake bottoms. But you still need it to travel.

"Going back till you got it right." If somehow you practiced often enough, you'd be able to perform properly, eliminate the mistakes of fingering, strike the right notes, find the best tempo. Still, you wouldn't have it right forever, you'd only have it right for then. Like musical scores, a life is subject to interpretation—even if you are the composer of your own. Getting it right, I've been suggesting, is also in part a collaborative activity—other people's memories help give you back your life, reshape your story, restart the memory process. Think about a high-school or college reunion, dredge up an old yearbook. See how you are memorialized there, what's scrawled under your picture (not to mention the picture itself, with which, try as you may, you cannot, or would rather not, coincide). Sometimes how others remember you draws a blank for you (and what is more painful than someone saying, "I remember you," when you don't remember her? the reverse, I suppose). But you may also have a blank filled in, restored by a fresh image, a forgotten name, a detail. Your life story is only as good as the last memoir you read.

That's why I devour memoirs the way some people read detective stories or thrillers. After all, there are crimes, mostly of the heart, and mysteries. Memoirs provide me with suspense of a different order. Will she stop falling in love with the wrong man, get a better job . . . sit down and write her poetry, her novel, or her memoir. Will you? You think, OK, her life is populated by famous and semifamous people; her life is glamorous or tragic. Your father wasn't a writer or a crook, just a lawyer or a businessman.

Your mother didn't drink or suffer from tuberculosis. You didn't grow up in Ceylon or, closer to home, Texas. You are not now, thank God, dying of breast cancer, or AIDS. But still, you can't help returning to your own life as if there were some magical, meaningful thread leading from the memoir writers to you. The six degrees of separation that mark the distance from your life to another's are really, as it turns out, degrees of connection. And my memoir is also about you.

2

Decades

I

Before Feminism: 1962–1968

> Ideally, one would be Simone de Beauvoir, smoking with
> Sartre at the Deux Magots, making an eccentric domestic
> arrangement that was secondary to important things and
> in their service. One would be poised, brilliant, equipped
> with a past, above the fray, beyond it, foreign not domes-
> tic. (And ideally Sartre would look like Albert Camus.)
> —Rachel M. Brownstein, *Becoming a Heroine*

It's 1962. I've just turned twenty-one in Paris. For my birthday, my
roommate at the Foyer International has given me a copy of the
Lettres portugaises, illustrated by Modigliani, and inscribed with a
message that invites me to consider how wonderful it is to be like
the *religieuse portugaise*—young and passionate—and concludes:
"dis 'fuck you' à tous les garçons [she was learning English from

the Americans who ate downstairs at the Foyer's student restaurant] et aime-les." Modigliani is an artist whose images of elongated women I find entrancing. I am knocked out by these letters. They are written, I believe then, by a real Portuguese nun, Mariana Alfocarado, seduced and abandoned by a real, if anonymous, Frenchman and obsessing about it. I identify completely, even though I'm of course not Portuguese (not to mention a nun). I have only begun to meet Frenchmen myself, and I can tell already that I'm out of my depth.

I'm also studying for my M.A. with the Middlebury Program in Paris and taking a yearlong seminar on Laclos. Antoine Adam, an authority on the early history of the novel in France, standing in front of the lectern in a huge amphitheater of the Sorbonne, produces a weekly lecture on *Les Liaisons dangereuses*. I'm supposed to write an essay on the novel; the choice of topic is up to me. The program has assigned me a tutor whose task it is to oversee the writing. I'll call him M. Souilliez. He lives on a dark street in the Latin Quarter, on a steep incline, near the Pantheon. It's April. A first draft of the *mémoire* is long overdue; I haven't begun the outline (the outline, "le plan," is at the heart of the French educational system). I have spent Christmas in Italy with an American boyfriend on a motorcycle; Easter vacation with my roommate at her home in Tunisia where I have discovered, among other things, the art of leg waxing with lemon and sugar. I don't know how I'm going to write this essay, let alone "le plan."

In despair I go to see the tutor one evening in his apartment. We sit in the living room and talk about *Les Liaisons dangereuses*; we talk, that is to say, about sex. I am inwardly panicked because I cannot come up with an essay topic, so I try to appear worldly and unconcerned, and with studied casualness hold forth on sex and love, and men and women. Suddenly, I get an idea: I'll write on the women in the novel, how each of them is betrayed by the images others have of them and that they each have of themselves. I sit at a table opposite M. Souilliez and start to make an outline. I'm inspired, excited. As I write, he gets up and walks around the room. I forget about him—I'm so happy that I at last have an idea! Then as I sit at the table, I feel a hand on my breast. M. Souilliez, standing behind my chair, has reached down and slipped his hand through my blouse around my left breast. I stop writing.

Despite the fact that I realize the moment I feel the hand feeling me that I have been chattering away about precisely these kinds of moves in the novel, it hasn't really occurred to me to make the connection between seduction (not to say sex) and M. Souilliez. I am now nonplussed. I try to imagine that in the *Liaisons*'s cast of characters I'm the sophisticated Madame de Merteuil, not the ingenue Cécile, even though I feel a lot more like a schoolgirl than a libertine (that's Cécile's problem in a nutshell, of course). I don't want to have to go to bed with M. Souilliez (he's "old" and not, I think, my type), but I also don't want a bad grade. The hand is still moving around inside the blouse. I remove the hand and sigh. "Oh, monsieur," I say, pausing and hoping for the world-weary tone of the Marquise in my best American jeune fille French, "j'ai déjà tant d'ennuis sans cela."

He goes no further, shrugs (in a Parisian gesture that seems to mean either it's your loss or you can't blame a guy for trying), and lets me leave. I race down the stairs out into the street and up the Boulevard St-Michel to the Foyer. When I get back to my room, I begin to wonder how much harm I've done myself. I finally write the essay—"Women and Love in *Les Liaisons dangereuses*: the Betrayal of Images"— and wait for the grade. The comments in the margins alternate between "b" *bien* and "md," *mal dit*. In general, I seem to have more insights than argumentative force. I take too long getting to the point: "what you say is true and interesting, but what's happened to your outline?" ("le plan"). I expect the quotations to do the work of commentary (they should play only a supporting role). And my favorite: "Never hesitate to be clear." In the light, I suppose, of these weaknesses, and despite a very nice overall comment (he thinks I'm smart), I get a mediocre grade on the essay (my own fault, I tell myself, for doing it all at the last minute; it really wasn't very good, anyway).

In 1968 when, having returned to New York, I decided to apply to graduate school, I went through my box marked "important papers" and discovered the M.A. essay. I looked at the grade on the title page, and it suddenly seemed to me (correctly, as it turned out) that the number grade (French style) was the equivalent not of the B on my transcript, but an A; the number had been mistranscribed. In 1968 it still didn't dawn on me to be angry about M. Souilliez's hand down my blouse. By then, flirting with a libertine incarnation of my own (I took the sexual revolution seriously), I congratulated myself instead, Merteuil-like, for having played the right card (didn't I get an A?). Recently, I ran into an old friend I knew when I was first living in Paris. I asked her if she remembered my scene with the tutor. "Oh yes," she said, "at the time we thought that sort of thing was flattering."

(In her book on Simone de Beauvoir, Judith Okely, who is exactly my age, described encounters with Frenchmen in Paris circa 1961 that seemed eerily familiar. I was struck by her account of spending the night—without losing her virginity, shades of a fifties casuistry—with a man who, "over breakfast" asked her "to read aloud the seduction scene from Laclos's *Les Liaisons Dangereuses*."[1])

I sometimes think that I have missed everything important to my generation: 1968 in Paris, 1968 at Columbia; the sixties really, although on my honeymoon in Ireland I did hear the Beatles sing on (pirate) Radio Caroline, "I Want to Hold Your Hand."

II

During Feminism: 1969–1977

> For words do not speak, while women do; as producers of signs, women can never be reduced to the status of symbols or tokens.
>
> —Claude Lévi-Strauss, *Structural Anthropology*

I'm in graduate school at Columbia, and feminism is in the streets . . . at least in a mainstream kind of way.

August 26, 1970, is the first annual nationwide "Women's Strike for Equality." Friends and I join the march down Fifth Avenue to celebrate the fiftieth anniversary of suffrage. Kate Millett publishes *Sexual Politics* and makes the cover of *Time Magazine*. At Town Hall it's Germaine Greer and a panel of women critics and writers (*The Female Eunuch* came out in the States in 1971) versus Norman Mailer. Mailer can't understand why women would become lesbians. After all, he opines, men can do to women what women do to each other—90 percent—and then some. In disgust, Jill Johnston walks off the stage and—to Mailer's despair: "C'mon Jill, be a lady"—embraces her lover in full view of the audience.

There is, in general, lots of writing and talk about female orgasm, how many (multiple, preferably), and what kind.

In January 1971, after reading an article by Vivian Gornick in the *New York Times Magazine* about consciousness-raising groups, some friends and I start our own group. At our first meeting we are amazed by our commonalities. In particular, we talk about how we don't want to be like our mothers who, we feel, did not know what they wanted. What do we want? The specifics are not clear, but the project involves taking charge of one's own life. It is nothing less than a fantasy of total control: not only having what we want but having it on our own terms and our timetable. The point of the group as we see it is to help each other bring this about: not to be victims.

What does this mean for graduate school? In graduate school, where the men are the teachers and the women the students, it's harder to say when things begin (certainly not in courses); it's more about things coming together—personally. One day the man who was to be the second reader on my dissertation, an eighteenth-century specialist, a man in his sixties, takes me aside to issue a dire warning: "Don't try to be another Kate Millett" (*Sexual Politics* was originally a Columbia English department Ph.D. thesis), "she wasn't first-rate to begin with." This man, who had coedited a popular anthology on the Enlightenment, taught a course on eighteenth-century French literature (from the anthology) in which, to see whether we had done the reading, he would pull questions out of a hat and match them with some hapless student. This had something to do with why I didn't want him as my adviser. But he did tell great stories: in fact, the account he gave of Julie de Lespinasse's life, the way a real woman (and a great letter writer) "died of love," sealed my fate: of course I was going to "be" in the eighteenth century.

In June 1972, fortified by our ongoing weekly discussions in the group, I take the plunge. I'm going to get serious about my work (no more reading, it's time, I'm thirty-one years old—old!): write the dissertation. (Actually, writing the dissertation seemed a solitary undertaking of such enormous moment that I withdrew from the group in order to "work." Holed up in a tiny room in a ground-floor tenement in the West Village, I wrote, cut off from the pleasure of the support that had gotten me there in the first place. I guess that was my idea of being a scholar—though I did turn to soap operas for relief.) I buy an electric typewriter; second-hand filing cabinets on Twenty-third Street, and a door that when placed on top of them makes a desk; I also declare my thesis topic: "Gender and Genre: An Analysis of Literary Femininity in the French and English 18th-Century Novel." In those days in the Columbia French department this is also called a stylistic structural analysis. I am going to analyze nine novels according to the principles of narratology and rhetoric: Propp and Greimas, Riffaterre and Genette, Barthes and Kristeva. I am going to do this, I say, as a feminist.

(Rereading these pages after having watched a three-hour profile on Richard M. Nixon on public television, I try to think about what—beyond marching and sit-ins—it might mean to have been writing a dissertation during the Vietnam War and Watergate. I learn, for instance, that on June 23, 1972, as I was, perhaps, drafting an introduction to "Gender and Genre," Richard Nixon was having a conversation with H. R. Haldeman about diverting the FBI. I easily remember spending hours glued to the Watergate proceedings in total fascination and indignation, but I seem to have made no visible *conceptual* connections between the preoccupations of my desk and the political upheaval of those public scenes.)

I had become a feminist and a structuralist together. That's a little condensed: this happened at the same time but on separate tracks. Feminism, for me, meant the group, *Ms. Magazine*, feminist fiction, and a whole set of what today we might more portentously call cultural practices. It meant a revolution in relationships—between women, between women and men—and one's perception of the real—in material and symbolic terms, even if we didn't talk that way. Feminism had to do with our lives. And yet despite pockets of local activity—the annual Barnard "Scholar and Feminist" conference, the occasional undergraduate offering—the academic institution was impervious to the dramatic changes occurring in social relations wrought by '68 and by feminism. Affirmative action began officially in 1972, but its immediate effects were almost invisible.

In 1972, as I remember things, the phrase "feminist criticism" was not yet an acknowledged working category, at least not on the fifth floor of Philosophy Hall where formalism reigned supreme. There was literary theory (what the good people did), and there was feminism (Kate Millett, English departments). I liked to think that criticism and feminism worked together. After all, I used to argue, both are modes of critique: the one of modes of criticism blind to their own assumptions about literature and art; the other of the ideology that regulates the relations between men and women in culture and society. It's hard to see now, but in the early seventies structuralism, as it was understood in American universities, like feminism seemed to mean a break with a reactionary past: the men's club model of lit crit. (In 1972 the name of the Men's Faculty Club, noted for its elegant Ladies' Lounge on the ground floor—the wives had to go somewhere, after all—was changed to the Faculty House.) For us, as beleaguered but ambitious graduate students, this "science of literature" was exciting; it provided a new language and a dream of transparency to sustain us in what we saw as a long struggle against "them." I can still remember the moment when in a study group I understood Saussure's model of the sign: never again would I confuse the word and the thing; literature and the world; sign and referent; signified and signifier (little knowing that Lacan, not to mention Derrida, had already turned this upside down).

33

This epiphany about the processes of signification was on a par only with the thrill of discovering binary oppositions and how they organize symbolic and social universes. Lévi-Strauss delivered the truth of this fact in person in the Barnard College gym in 1972 (poststructuralism, with a whole new set of emphases, had already unsettled structuralism in France, but colonials necessarily live according to belated cadences). What I mainly remember from this event was the conviction (Lévi-Strauss's, then rapidly mine) that binary oppositions were embedded functionally in the brain. For me, it all went together perfectly with Beauvoir's magisterial analyses of the polarizing operations that opposed man as Same to woman as Other (Beauvoir herself, of course, seriously engaged with Lévi-Strauss's paradigms); and even, since everything made sense in these vast systems, with the lowly housewife's "click," the codes of domestic oppression that Jane O'Reilly famously deciphered in *Ms. Magazine*'s spring 1972 preview issue. Whatever the cultural material, structuralist models of analysis rescued you from the murk of ambiguity (not to say personal confusion) and privileged authority (the variously tweeded "we's" of a fifties' legacy), and feminism showed you what to make of what you found. Between the capacious categories of narratology and the stringent lines of feminist hermeneutics, there was no text the new "we" couldn't crack. It was a heady moment.

Is it true that there was no problem in articulating feminism and structuralism together? Yes and no. It's probably that combination of enthusiasms that British reviewers of the book (about French and English eighteenth-century novels) my thesis finally became— *The Heroine's Text* (1980)—found so deadly: structuralist jargon and feminist ideology. I kept seeing the same story everywhere, they complained. Well, yes, that's the whole point (which American academics—at least the feminist ones—generally got): heroines either die (it's true that Madame de Merteuil survives, but she's exiled and hideously disfigured) or marry (sometimes both, like Rousseau's Julie). The objections to my language (I called these endings "dysphoric" and "euphoric") and approach (plot summary, as the unkinder put it) bothered me less (even if they were insulting and sort of true) than a certain feminist refusal of the project for "ideological" reasons. There were those who felt (1) that all formalism was male, hence incompatible with feminist analysis, and (2) that the task of feminism was to respond to the issues of "real" women. In that sense I was indeed guilty as charged. Women were strikingly absent from my dissertation. When I chose the expression "literary femininity," I meant it to mark my distance from anything real and to sound theoretically advanced (to ward off the ambient disdain that "working on women" generated): women in fiction, but with an emphasis on narrative; female destiny, with an emphasis on plot. This was my way of showing (again) my difference both from Kate Millett, the incarnation of "strident" feminism, and from the mode of "images of women" that had already begun to emerge in English studies. Any historical considerations were necessarily foreclosed. On the one hand, the historical seemed like an antiquated belief in the referent; on the other, the invocation of the historical as the truth value of literature, the dominant mode of eighteenth-century studies, was the very thing I wanted most to escape from and oppose.

In 1972 my corpus, as we then called it, was made up entirely of respected male authors, major figures (with the exception of the bad boys Sade and Cleland, forgiven because of outrageousness and sex), and famous books. It was the canon, although the term wasn't current at that point. And women authors? The entire time I was a graduate student, during lectures, reading for seminars, for the thesis, I never once asked myself the question of female authorship, despite the fact that I must have read some women writers for course work or exams: Marie de France, Louise Labé, Marie-Madeleine de Lafayette, Germaine de Staël (the last two known then of course as Mme de . . .). Besides, by the time I started writing my dissertation, the Author (male) was Dead, intentions a fallacy, and all I cared about was The Text. I blamed—if I blamed— texts, not authors, for the representation of women. And not even texts: texts were prisoners of ideology just as men were prisoners of sex.

After my thesis defense it was reported to me that the sole

woman on the jury (one of Columbia's classic tokens) had praised me for "sitting on my feelings." I've never been absolutely sure what that meant: that I was (tautologically) angry because feminist, but my writing was cool and "scientific"? Or that through the elaborate veils of my narratological tables she could tell I really cared. About what? About the logic of "female plot" that killed off heroines—exquisite cadavers as I called them in my first article—at the story's close?

What I really cared about then, I think, had as much to do with my own fate as with the fictional destiny of women in the eighteenth-century novel. At stake, if buried, in the ponderous prose of my structuralist feminism was the story of *my* plot: my own "coming to writing"—"as a woman"—to invoke the language of a feminist literary criticism that was to flower after the mid-seventies. Despite the hierarchies and abuses of academic conventions, then, I saw writing a dissertation as something radical but also literary: as becoming the heroine of my life. Despite the so-called feminization of the profession, my getting a Ph.D. in the early seventies felt like a violation of gender expectations. In 1961, having gathered my ideas about appropriate intellectual and domestic arrangements in the America of the late fifties, it seemed natural for my college boyfriend to get a doctorate (even if that was hardly his—nor indeed our generation's—idea of creative accomplishment); I was slated to get an M.A. and teach high-school French, unless, of course—my mother's fifties' fantasy for me—I married very well and got to be a woman of leisure who spoke French only in Europe. When, a decade later, I started writing and saw the pages pile up on my desk—a lot of the time spent at my desk involved admiring the *height* of the chapters—it seemed miraculous—as though someone else were responsible for producing the work. The man I lived with at the time, who had mixed emotions about my passion for the enterprise, did a drawing of me sitting with my hands thrown up in the air, as if in astonishment, watching the pages—produced by my cat pounding away at the typewriter—fly upward with a life of their own. But when my typist met me with the final version of the manuscript, I burst into uncontrollable tears on Broadway at 116th Street: I suppose that's part of what I was "sitting on" during the defense.

Part, but not the whole story. I was not, of course, merely a tearful heroine overcome by the events taking place around her. I was also the author of her destiny. I had a very clear sense of having done the work and wanting to own it. And so, in 1973, inspired by the example of Judy Chicago, I renamed myself. I had been using my ex-husband's name—I married briefly and unhappily in the mid-sixties—and the idea of seeing the signifier of my misery embossed on my diploma seemed suddenly and thoroughly unacceptable. At the same time, the idea of returning to my father's (also my "maiden") name seemed regressive. Not bold enough to go all the way and call myself Nancy New York, or to pick a name that pleased me out of the phone book, I took my mother's name, Miller. It was not lost on me that this was still to take a man's—my grandfather's—name or that I was taking the name of my worthiest adversary, my mother. Despite these contradictions, it seemed the perfect solution.

(Not my grandfather's real name either, which according to some family legends may have been Middlarsky, but the Ellis Island rendition of an immigrant's desire to be a "Yankee." I kept my father's name Kipnis as my legal middle name and made the initial K part of my new signature. My father, who was a lawyer, took care of the legal formalities for me and never said how he felt about the change. My dissertation director, however, who took the conventions of the patriarchy very seriously, was, to my great amusement, shocked. The woman typing my thesis, a student at General Studies, who was rapidly changing her life, changed her name too, and I felt quite pleased to have inspired her to do it.)

I will admit to a certain nostalgia for the gestures of those years in feminism that we have now come to take for granted, like being called Ms. I sometimes long for the conviction we had then that changing the language counted for something.

III

Feminist Literary Criticism: 1978–1989

And why don't you write? Write! Writing is for you, you
are for you; your body is yours, take it.
—Hélène Cixous, "The Laugh of the Medusa"

By the fall of 1978, when after having taught my first graduate
course—a seminar—on (French) women authors, I wrote
"Emphasis Added" (the second of my essays on women's writing),
I had both regressed to and returned from the Portuguese nun. I
had fully lived out Simone de Beauvoir's analysis of the *grande
amoureuse*—the woman hopelessly and desperately in love—and
changed literatures. I wrote this essay, which takes its examples
from Lafayette's *Princess of Clèves* and Eliot's *Mill on the Floss*, in
total solitude, in the aftermath of a story with a Frenchman that
had turned out badly (let's just say that I had renunciation thrust
upon me). When I discovered, by teaching the letters in a course
on women writers, that the Portuguese nun was really a man (a
literary hack) in drag, I was more embarrassed at my ignorance, I
think, than disappointed. Besides, I didn't need her anymore: I
didn't need to be in love with a man to write. That was half of
the story; the other half was falling in love with the Princess of
Clèves: the heroine and the novel.

When I say that I fell in love I mean both that this book swept
me away and that it took me somewhere. Working on "Emphasis
Added" six years after starting to write my dissertation was like
a second coming to writing. The dissertation was still sitting on
my desk waiting to be revised, transformed (one hoped) into the
tenure book. It seemed to me that I needed to do another kind
of writing in order to talk about women writers; but the old task
demanded its due, and the two projects were at odds with each
other. As it turned out, it was writing the new essay that allowed
me to finish the old book, to finish off a certain past with the

flourish of an epilogue. Those few pages are the only part of that book I can still bear to read.

I wrote the epilogue to *The Heroine's Text* in a single sitting, in rage against an anonymous and extremely hostile (female) reader's report. I wish, or I think I wish, I still had a copy of the report. As I recollect it, the reader complained, among other things, that I didn't seem to realize that the novels I analyzed were written by men. This felt at the time an outrageous objection to make to me, of all people! Still, I had to ponder the remark, and it led me to make the point explicitly at the close of the book: that these novels were written by men for men through the double fiction of the female reader and her heroine. It also led me to think about my complete failure to consider what difference women's fictions would have made to my argument. That was a point less easily fixed. It seems to me now that a lot of the energy that fueled my writing after the epilogue came from a desire for reparation: How could I not have taken female authorship into account from the beginning?

(At the end of the decade, through one of the rare institutional arrangements at Columbia that—inadvertently—worked on behalf of women, I met Carolyn Heilbrun, then a senior member of the English Department, who performed several small miracles that saved both my writing and my career. We twice taught a seminar together, called "The Heroine's Text," in which we read French and English, male- and female-authored novels and tried to figure out—only occasionally agreeing—whether the limited arrangements of female plot turned out differently either in national tradition or according to authorial gender.)

Once I started working on women writers and on feminist criticism as literary theory, I felt myself to be instantly losing status. Not within the feminist community at large, of course, but within the little world of French departments that I was used to. (I'm still not sure whether this is true, or just what I worried about.) No doubt this anxiety was also bound up with the fact that at the same time I began to "leave the century": what would it mean not to "have" a period? But that is the matter of another reflection about the organization of literary studies.

(At a departmental party one day, I was deep in conversation with a female colleague. We were interrupted by a male colleague, who asked what we were talking about. When we foolishly revealed the truth about the subject of our absorption—our hair-cuts, we go to the same haircutter—he was jubilant: "Oh," he said, "I always wondered what women talked about when they were alone." I guess I didn't look at him as witheringly as I had hoped since he went on to pursue his interruption. Did I, he wanted to know, have a period? Being what is called "perimenopausal" at the time, I had to work very hard not to answer in terms of my newly haywire cycle. I censored my "sometimes" and said no, since he was merely looking, as it turned out, for someone specialized in the right historical period to serve on an orals committee. But it's true that not having a period in academia can be a problem.)

At one point a feminist critic brought me up against this anxiety of authority as we were returning from a conference in which I had given a paper on women's autobiography: "You've always worked on women, haven't you?" she asked. Male authors, I thought, but she had my number: in the shadows of their charac-ters, *women* all the same. I never would be taken seriously. Still, if I had always been a feminist in my work on male writers, "working on women" seemed to make me into a different (read "lower") order of feminist: soft instead of hard, marginal instead of central. Nonetheless, that was where I was going; nor was I alone. For me to have resisted the turn to women's writing would perhaps require greater explanation than my seduction by it. Despite, or perhaps because of the excitement, even the scandal, of *Sexual Politics* and the success of Judith Fetterley's *The Resisting Reader* in 1978, the trend in feminist literary studies in the late seventies was moving massively toward the study of women's writing, summarized in the title of Elaine Showalter's 1977 *A Literature of Their Own*.

Again, I am struck with the difficulty and strangeness of evok-ing a time when just *saying* "women's writing" had a radical edge to it. When I began to "work on women" in the late seventies, I had no idea of what that was going to mean for me and more generally for developments in feminist theory. In personal terms it meant a new sense of self-authorization that changed my relation to all the issues in the profession—especially to "theory"—and changed my identity within it. I think this is because in North American feminist criticism, by an interesting process of slippage, authorial subjectivity (itself implicitly constructed on the model of the heroine) became another way of talking about female agency. Through these effects of substitution, it became possible for me, a reader of novels (alternately, a critical heroine), to cast myself (at least in my own eyes) as a feminist theorist. Or so it seemed at the time. By the early eighties, the literary appropriation of feminist theory had been accomplished. This process, which can be tracked, if a little too neatly, by two titles that seem to echo each other—*Madwoman in the Attic* (1979) and *Honey-Mad Women* (1988)—was emblematic of the decade's intellectual style. Although differences of position separate these two powerful works, their authors, Sandra Gilbert and Susan Gubar on the one hand, and Patricia Yaeger, on the other, all rely importantly on interwoven metaphors of literary identity and female experience to make their case. (It's my sense that the appeal of literary metaphors waned in the nineties, along with the attrition of an earlier confidence in figures of gender altogether.)

The eighties also saw the widespread formalization of women's studies programs, many of which had come into being throughout the United States in the late seventies. In 1981, when I moved across the street from Columbia to Barnard as the director of their fledgling Women's Studies Program, it seemed to me (and this was part of what allowed me to take an administrative job that I was otherwise unprepared for) that the rise of feminist scholarship as an institutional force derived at least in part from the sense of collective authorization that "working on women" provided. From my office with the decorator-purple (we hoped subversive) walls, I wrote a book-length collection of memos, characterized by the rhetorical turns of feminist righteousness, demanding courses, and lines in a mode a colleague from Political Science taught me called "bullets"; my memo style, she explained, was too narrative.

By 1985, however, that interlocking sense of personal conviction and political solidarity—speaking "as a feminist" *for all women*—had already begun to erode within the feminist community. This was the moment when white mainstream feminists finally began to pay attention to internal divisions that of course had been there from the beginning. The publication, for instance, in 1981 of *This Bridge Called My Back: Writings by Radical Women of Color* clearly marks the terms of dissent from the discourse of unity. By 1985, the date I assign only somewhat arbitrarily to this crisis, women of color refused a definition of feminism that by the whiteness of its universal subject did not include them, and poststructuralist critics looked suspiciously upon a binary account of gender with referential claims. Did we really want to posit a *female* experience as the ground of women's identity? Not to be left out, mainstream academics (male and female), who saw themselves as upholders of literary standards, trounced feminist critics for confusing aesthetics and sociology. Couldn't we tell art from women? This last position, which continued to thrive in the nineties, in many ways announces the colors of the fifties: a return to a Cold War ideology that takes the form on the academic front of an entwined belief in Art and the Individual.

IV

After Feminism? 1990–

Bob Dylan is clearly the first rock-and-roller to reach 50 as a meaningful artist.

   —Dave Marsh, *New York Times*, May 19, 1991

I became a feminist critic along with a certain history—as it was being made around me. By this I mean that my decades of intellectual formation coincided with those of another chronology, a chronology of social revolution. I said earlier that I had missed '68. That's true if we think of '68 narrowly as a single apocalyptic event or even as a network of events with specific locales: the Sorbonne, Berkeley, Columbia. But '68, we know, can also be seen as a trope: the figure of diffuse political movements, including feminism, that came to restructure the social repertoire of cultural images. In this sense '68 didn't miss me.

Teresa de Lauretis has argued that feminism's unique method was what in the United States we referred to as "consciousness-raising" and that she prefers to call, through translation back from Italian, the practice of "self-consciousness." And certainly it was in the space of this group work that I began for the first time to make sense of my life as a good daughter of the patriarchy. What flowered from those moments and flashes of insight were the elements of an analysis—a reading—that would make a larger kind of sense when articulated collectively. The decades of the seventies and eighties saw the invention of new social subjects, critics and readers who, in the cultural aftermath of '68, created the feminism we now look back on. Whether one calls this the institutionalization or, as I prefer, the textualization of feminism, what matters is the fact of that construction: the library of feminism's literatures.

But, you may say, this sounds so elegiac, as though what matters to you were solely the invention of feminism's noble past or, worse, its future anterior: what feminism will have been. It's true. . . . At fifty, like Lot's wife, I seemed rigidly turned toward the past. What had I left behind? Despite the fashion look-alikes, it's not the sixties, and I don't have to worry about M. Souilliez's hand down my blouse. It's not the seventies, and I don't have to hide my rage in writing from my judges. It's not the eighties, and I'm not running a women's studies program. Still, you point out, sexual harassment is an ever-present feature of academic life for students and, like Charlotte Brontë's feisty heroine Lucy Snowe, our younger colleagues continue to find their authority challenged. You're just giving us a personal narrative of escape from certain penalties of youth and a more vulnerable professional location; what is it exactly that you miss?

I confess: I look back wistfully to the seventies and the extraordinary conjunction of structuralism and feminism that fed both my writing and my life. But, most of all, I miss the passion of community (what we took for community), as well as our belief that things would change. In the conclusion to *Conflicts in Feminism* the editors, Marianne Hirsch and Evelyn Fox Keller, writing on the threshold of the nineties, expressed their separate views in facing columns meant to be seen as a conversation between them, two signatures allowing for their own differences. Evelyn Fox Keller described her attachment to this period: "If I were to name one feature of feminist theorizing in the seventies for which I am openly nostalgic, it is the conviction then widely held that there was important work to be done—work that could be supported in the name of feminism not because all feminists held the same priorities, but because that work had a radical thrust from which, we believed, feminists—and women—would generally gain some benefit."[2] The loss to contemporary feminism of the energy that emerged from those beliefs cannot be underestimated, even if the reasons for political alignments within feminism and between feminism and other social movements were pressing. Keller concluded her thought about these internal conflicts by looking ahead to a possible future for feminism in which debate might lead to renewal rather than decline, as well as to an "ethic of criticism": "We have learned well the lesson that differences can be suppressed; I suggest we need also to learn that commonalities can be as facilely denied as they were once assumed" (384–85). But what would be the grounds of new commonalities among women in a postfeminist age?

Having arrived at that point, I might have adopted a more confident, visionary tone and scanned the cultural firmament for signs of things to come: portents for feminism after its civil wars. But that would have required that I felt either prepared to speak for feminism or willing, as I had been on so many occasions, to predict what its next moves might and should be. I wasn't. I was more at ease reviewing, even teaching, the history of a feminist past.

Against the backdrop of magazine headlines announcing the death of feminism, the hoopla surrounding "The Year of the

Woman" in electoral politics, and media-enhanced rejections of second-wave feminists by younger women, feminism in the nineties indeed proved to be full of the internal conflicts already at work in the eighties.[3] It was a time of struggles between generations about who represented feminism and how—of misunderstandings, recriminations, and missed opportunities for dialogue.

It became painful to speak as a feminist in public, and I mainly fell silent.

But as it turned out, it was precisely through my inability to assume the feminist position as if it were mine that feminism came back to me in another voice—a voice at once more personal and more curious about what else in the years that preceded feminism had brought me (and other women like me) to rename myself.

Circa 1959

> I forced myself to keep my own figure fictitious; leg-
> endary. If I had said, Look here am I uneducated, because
> my brothers used up all the family funds which is the
> fact—Well theyd have said; she has an axe to grind; and no
> one would have taken me seriously.
> —Virginia Woolf (letter to Ethel Smyth, June 8, 1933)

I

The Con: A Fable

I didn't go to Stratford-upon-Avon to study Shakespeare. That's not
true either. I did want to study Shakespeare. I was an English major,
after all. But mainly I wanted to get away from my parents and
impress my boyfriend. David had given me a brown leather-bound
diary with gilt-tipped pages for a going-away present. As soon as
the boat pulled out of the harbor, I started recording my feelings
and impressions. After some twenty pages, the diary abruptly stops
with an arrow pointing toward Oxford. Not another line. And yet
what happened at Oxford was the beginning of everything, which
of course I couldn't possibly have known then. It was 1959, and I
was eighteen—a literary girl in love with books (her boyfriend was
an English major too).

The Shakespeare Institute offered a six-week summer course for foreign students. I had begun reading Henry James and admired Isabel Archer. It took a while for me to understand that being an American in England was being a foreigner. I knew this; I just hadn't made the connection. Famous Shakespeareans gave lectures at the institute every morning. On performance nights we would go to The Dirty Duck, the pub across the road from the Royal Shakespeare Theatre, and wait for the actors to turn up. Our teachers chatted with them about the performance, almost casually over rounds of lager. We watched them out of the corner of our eyes. Was I impressed? I note my views in my diary, on July 25, 1959: "Stratford: is a phony, artificial, contrived TOURIST TOWN. It is quaint but this really isn't enough." Bored by school from the beginning, I wrote home daily aerograms complaining to my parents. Couldn't I please drop my classes and travel all summer?

Dearest Doll, my father begins. Then comes a summary of paternal permissions and prohibitions:

1. The fees have been paid. Receipt is dated July 6.
2. You may rent a bike and ride it.
3. You may travel week-ends. Be discreet.
4. Tuition covers whole period. Don't judge course by partial early performance.
5. Passage back has been assured and extension of stay is out of question.

My father was one of the last patriarchs and a lawyer to boot.

One weekend my parents, who were touring Northern Europe, came to England, and I took the train to meet them in London. There's a picture my father snapped on an excursion to Whitechapel we made together that weekend. I'm standing with my mother, wearing a navy blue print sleeveless dress that has a tight dropped waist with a matching bolero jacket (fig. 3.1). My frizzy hair (the bane of my existence) is pulled back tight in a bun, and I'm wearing prescription sunglasses, light green lenses with pale, almost transparent pink harlequin frames that cast a V-like shadow on my cheeks. In the diary I describe the unsmiling girl in

FIG. 3.1. My mother and me.
Photograph by my father, Louis Kipnis.

the picture as she appeared a few weeks earlier that summer on the SS *Rotterdam* where I documented my experiments in shipboard romance. "Tonight I feel ugly. I've noticed this for some time. My figure looked quite good in the navy dress but there is something wrong with my face." I seemed to be having a hard time having fun, even without the company of my parents.

One day toward the end of the summer course, Judy, another American girl in our group at Stratford, and I hitchhiked to Oxford. The Bodleian and the Radcliffe Camera were high on the list that David had compiled for my instruction, though he had not yet crossed the ocean himself (not that we were rivalrous). A large part of my desire to visit Oxford was to report on what I had seen with as much architectural detail as I could muster (though never as much as he required). In the late afternoon, standing morosely under our umbrellas in the parking lot of one of the colleges, Judy and I were approached by a man in a long trench coat who asked if we needed help. A lecturer at King's College, just back from teaching in the States (Yale, no less), with an invitation to return was how Peter Bradshaw presented himself. Americans had been very kind to him during his stay, he said, and he wanted to repay their generosity. Besides, he casually added on the way to the car, his family had their ancestral home, a castle, in Warwick, a town not far from Stratford. As we drove back in the rain, we made plans for the following week. Judy and I were to visit his chateau and meet his family. (Our children, I thought happily in the backseat, will have an English accent.) One night, after a week of meals and drinks, we all went back to one of the student's rooms to drink Scotch, a newly acquired taste for me. Peter explained that he couldn't drive back to Warwick that night because his car was being repaired. I eagerly offered him my room, proposing to sleep with Judy and her roommate in theirs.

Flash forward. Reader, please remember this is the fifties, we cut away from the bedroom to which I returned in stealth later that night. (It's also true that I can't see into that room anymore, beyond twin beds, a tall dresser, and a proliferation of ruffles and anti-macassars.) The next morning, unable to concentrate on the lecture, and fantasizing about our romantic adventures to come—the castle, the moat—I reread the week's mail. My parents had finally sent me the money I'd been pleading for, and I wanted to count it again. The envelope was empty. A small rush of panic made me sweaty. I turned to Judy: look in your wallet, I signaled wildly in pantomime. She gestured back that her money was gone too. Abandoning Coriolanus to his fate, we jumped up in tandem, hopped on our bikes, and raced back to our rooms at the Barwyn. No money anywhere. It wasn't quite 1 p.m.

The afternoon dragged on. I felt sure my prince would return. So when the police arrived at tea time, called in by one of the other students who had disapproved of "Peter" from the start, I refused to talk. (Once back in Stratford, Peter had shared meals with us, sometimes treating us to drinks, all the while politely cadging small sums of money from the students in our little group; quietly, one-by-one, each promising not to tell the others.) The officers were polite and kind—they were English, after all, but unbending. They threatened to tell our parents if we didn't cooperate. My parents will kill me, I thought, and in my case this was barely a figure of speech. I nodded when I had to admit in front of everyone that there were "intimacies" between Peter and me, but I did not confess that he had proposed to me; the marriage proposal seemed the final humiliation rather than a mitigating excuse. We traipsed down to the police station at the edge of the village and grudgingly flipped through an album of mug shots, convinced that this was a huge, not to say, unjust waste of our time, that Peter would reappear as promised—a gentleman's word.

We begged the policeman to phone him. But there was no Bradshaw teaching at King's College. Not only was the family not titled, its name didn't exist in Warwick. The worst was yet to come. I turned a page, and my heart, as they say, stood still. Full face or in profile, I don't remember which, there was the face I had spent the night in bed with; but despite the evidence I still would not admit to myself that I had been caressed by a criminal. "Peter" had recently been released from prison. I was a nice Jewish girl from New York who went to midnight concerts at Carnegie Hall and saw only foreign movies in black and white. How could I have day-dreamed about life with a man who had spent most of his doing time for conning little old ladies?

Reader, did I really want to marry him? True, I wanted an adventure, but then I couldn't manage to separate it from fairy tale—lords, castles, being picked up out of your boring middle-class life and carried away to reign as the princess (eventually queen) you really were. The professor would have to stand in for the prince, the white car for the horse. I was still in the world of fifties' girls where, whatever your ambition—to be smart, learn about Shakespeare, travel the world—that desire was usually harnessed to the marriage plot. I don't remember leaving Stratford, but once I got to Paris, I closed the door on England and my stupid American girl secret and changed my major to French. In the summer of 1959 I had already found my emotional style—a kind of desperate unknowing.

II

Black Stockings

> Sexual intercourse began
> In nineteen sixty-three
> (Which was rather late for me)—
> Between the end of the *Chatterley* ban
> And the Beatles' first LP.
> —Philip Larkin, "Annus Mirabilis"

At the beginning of the 1990s I was invited to contribute to an anthology that asked its contributors to answer the question: How did you become a feminist literary critic?[1] The editors describe the project as "an effort of remembering and historicizing, a collection of individual stories that, taken together, comprise a collective story—histories that make a history" (1). These stories form an intellectual memoir emerging from a generation of American women with literary aspirations for whom the 1950s were "the decade that produced us and produced feminism" (2)—"us," that is to say, academics, at various points on the graph of their middle age; most straight and white and writing in the nineties from tenured positions. My piece of the group memoir was titled "Decades," where the sixties' prelude to my seventies' coming-to-feminism story began, as it happened, in Paris. Ten years later I found myself writing what feels like the prequel to "Decades"; but this time returning to the native grounds of my New York fifties, to the years and yearnings that directly preceded the official narrative.

But which fifties and whose? If there is a rough consensus about how to date the moment at which the fifties seemed over, it's of course in large part due to the magnitude of the presidential assassination in 1963. Less easy to pinpoint as traumatically, the beginning of its end. We could take the 1957 launching of Sputnik or, on the literary scene, the stunning success of Jack Kerouac's *On the Road*. For autobiographical reasons, as we've seen, I'm partial to 1959, when I first went to Europe and began, unbeknownst to me, of course, my feminist odyssey—fear of flying when we were still crossing the ocean by boat. The crossing changed my life. In 1959 the Barbie doll, weird harbinger of feminine futures and bodies, appeared on the scene. In 1959 Castro became premier of Cuba. Such are the intimacies of the time line.

Whatever shape you give to the arc of postwar culture, there's evidence in this period of transition pointing to a palpable if undefinable sense that in the realm of the social relations between men and women, but especially for American women, things were changing. *The Presidential Report on the Status of Women*, the result of the work of Kennedy's Commission on the Status of Women established in 1961, made front-page news in 1963. With predictable ambiguity the report addressed questions about what were not then called gender roles and the social implications of women's work. And furtively but surely, ideas about what sex might mean for women were in the air. In 1960 the Pill was approved by the FDA. By 1963 more than two million American women were taking the Pill, and their numbers were rising. The "problem without a name" described by Betty Friedan had everything to do with sex: "Sex," she argues, "is the only frontier open to women who have always lived within the confines of the feminine mystique. In the past fifteen years, the sexual frontier has been forced to expand perhaps beyond the limits of possibility, to fill the time available, to fill the vacuum created by denial of larger goals and purposes for American women" (261).[2] A radical social refiguration for girls took place in this window between Kerouac and Kennedy, Barbie and Betty, but what road could an adventurous girl follow? Sylvia Plath—an emblematic though not perhaps exemplary figure of the drama lived by ambitious girls of this era—Sylvia Plath left for England with Ted Hughes at the end of 1959 and killed herself in London in February 1963.

In the spring of 1959 I was a sophomore at Barnard College, Columbia University's college for women. This was the year that Allen Ginsberg and his friends read their new poetry at Columbia University and got lots of attention. When she described the event in the *Partisan Review*, Diana Trilling looked down disdainfully from her perch as faculty wife with reserved seats at the girls who turned out for Ginsberg's performance—"the always-new shock of so many young girls, so few of them pretty, and so many dreadful black stockings." She did not think much of our male counterparts either—"so many young men, so few of them—despite the many black beards—with any promise of masculinity" (224). Nonetheless, she was forced to admit that the audience of such poor specimens didn't smell bad![3]

This was one of two major national events related to the Columbia scene that year. The second had to do with the famous literary Van Doren family. Mark Van Doren was retiring, but the possibility of continuity was present in the form of his son Charles, who was just finishing his Ph.D. and had been newly promoted to the rank of assistant professor. Father and son had shared an office; now Charlie was to be on his own. But Charlie let the family down in a big way. He allowed himself to be seduced by a deal with NBC television to appear on the enormously popular quiz show, *Twenty-One*. Van Doren's dazzling success as a contestant conferred instant national celebrity. But when his picture appeared on the cover of *Life* magazine in October 1959, it was not just because he was smart. *Twenty-One* had been rigged, and Van Doren admitted his guilty role before a House subcommittee in Washington. Because it was about television—a young medium that inspired both fear and enchantment—and because Van Doren was a Van Doren, exposure was relentless. Charles Van Doren withdrew from Columbia and, for a long while, from the public eye. (This story was revived in the nineties by the movie *Quiz Show*.)

What does this American fable of lost innocence have to do with my own, you might be wondering? For one thing, Charlie's "last and favorite" student (his words) was none other than David, my very own Renaissance man, whom we saw from afar in the Stratford episode, a senior at Columbia, forever ahead of me. Let these few degrees of separation provide a metaphorical bridge to the snapshot of an era. That connection, I figure, makes it my story too. I seem to have been close to what turned out to have mattered, what made history; but somehow I was always at an oblique (girl's?) angle to the real thing. David went to the poetry reading, he says; why didn't he take me? I thought we went everywhere important together. Suddenly this event that I don't remember seems symptomatic. What else did I miss?

The *Life* magazine photo spread on the Van Dorens shows a clan of WASP (*avant la lettre*) entitlement where, whatever else women may have accomplished—and many of the Van Doren women were "literary" too—they are of course called "Mrs. Charles Van Doren" or, my favorite, "Mrs. Spencer Klaw." Babies are ubiquitous, even when the women have professional activities to their names. The men are the professors. In one photo Charlie is sitting around a seminar table, index finger raised ominously, warning the class of all male students "to expect a question on Milton in the M.A. exam." In another father and son bond in a book-lined office, talking of literature and baseball. Under the photo of Charlie's wife "dandling" their baby daughter, the caption explains that he "hired her as secretary to answer his *Twenty-One* fan mail and married her three months later."

Life or *Life* magazine? If marrying literary royalty was not the destiny that the girls in their "dreadful black stockings" had in mind, it's what framed their universe. Female ambition was rarely on display in its own form or even visible to ourselves—not that we saw ourselves self-consciously as a group. On the contrary. This was the era of individual rebellions. The contingency that links the Van Doren scandal to the scene at the poetry reading makes another kind of sense when replaced in a retrospective narrative about a piece of Manhattan culture in the 1950s. But what *is* memory, if not a reconstruction?

In her memoir about coming of age in this urban landscape, Hettie Jones recalls Trilling's *Partisan* article with an amused edge: "She didn't find us pretty, and hadn't liked our legs at all. 'So many blackest black stockings,' she wrote with distaste." But there's a nice twist to this recollection. A year later Hettie, who worked as a subscription manager at the magazine, encounters Mary McCarthy at a party. " 'I like your stockings,' " McCarthy says with a smile. Jones couldn't keep herself from telling the writer where she could buy them herself: "on Fourteenth Street, at the Bargain Hosiery Center next to the Catholic Church" (129).[4]

III

Did "Bad" Sex Produce "Good" Feminism?
Or, How Did We Get to the Seventies?

> So I began to think maybe it was true that when you were married and had children it was like being brainwashed, and afterward you went about numb as a slave in some private, totalitarian state.
>
> —Sylvia Plath, *The Bell Jar*

What if you didn't want to marry the prince, or anyone else for that matter?

Looking, in a short history of literary criticism, at the sixties as they modulate into the seventies, Catharine Stimpson returns to the period in which Kate Millett's *Sexual Politics* came into existence, evoking that era as a personal witness to it, the mid-sixties when both Kates were teaching at Barnard.

> Kate and I wanted to be accepted in the academy that we treasured, to have our degrees and lecterns. We also wanted to be different. Ambition, not the desire to marry the boy next door, had taken Kate out of Saint Paul, Minnesota, and me out of Bellingham, Washington. Within a few weeks, we were sharing an office at Barnard. She looked more conservative than I, in her long skirts, pumps, and hair drawn back in, yes, a bun. I jumped around the corridors in miniskirts, tights, and unruly, unkeyed, naturally curly locks. The discrepancy between a woman's decorous appearance and flaring subjectivity—in a Jane Eyre, for example—was to become a theme for feminist criticism. I might have looked the more radical, but I was, intellectually, the more conservative, prudent, and buttoned-up. (252)

Her account, Stimpson notes half-apologetically, while "autobiographical," nonetheless "reflects some of the cultural ferment in which feminist criticism developed" (251).[5] But for me, it's precisely the personal details of skirts, hair, shoes that make cultural history come alive: the inclusion of those daily issues of *style* that define a moment in a collective social pattern; pantyhose and tights have replaced the black stockings. (Hettie Jones dates the discovery of tights as part of the all-black uniform to the post-Sputnik fall of 1961, to "Goldin Dance Supply on Eighth Street," where you could buy "dirt-defying, indestructible tights . . . made only for dancers then and only in black—which freed you from fragile nylon stockings and the cold, unreliable, metal clips of a garter belt" [46]). I love having the hair and the skirts in my line of vision.

Writing in the 1990s and providing the intellectual history of a young feminist from a post-fifties' generation, Jane Gallop personalizes the sexual in sexual politics. She describes the effect of reading *The Second Sex* in the early 1970s; she learned from Beauvoir's essay, she says, that women could masturbate. Then she went on to be fired up by her studies in college and graduate school; not surprisingly, she wrote her dissertation on Sade (4).[6] (Female perversions, we know, often begin in school.) What turned Beauvoir on? In the spring of 1997 the love letters Simone de Beauvoir wrote in English to Nelson Algren were published in France—translated into French by Sylvie Le Bon de Beauvoir, Beauvoir's adopted daughter and literary executor. The letters, now available in the original English, begin in 1947 after Beauvoir's visit to America during the early stages of writing the essay that was to become *The Second Sex*.[7] In France the importance of the letters was discussed in a popular television program ("Bouillon de Culture," March 6, 1997) devoted to contemporary writers—all men. A woman editor (and the only woman on the screen, including the host) from Gallimard, the publisher, who assured the viewers that men could be interested in this aspect of Beauvoir's life too, presented the letters. Philippe Sollers, the ubiquitous French man of letters, remarked with his usual authority that we would now be able to understand *The Second Sex* in a new way since we can see that it was thanks to her love for Algren that Beauvoir was empowered to write *The Second Sex*—thus proving that the book wasn't the "catechism for feminists" it had been made out to be. In 1947 Beauvoir discovers America, orgasm, and writes a major book. "We must put dates on things," Sollers remarks, as though he had just discovered America himself.

Reviewers were especially enchanted by places in which Beauvoir showed she was "just a woman" like all the rest of us, a hot heterosexual woman, not an amoral existentialist and lesbian. "But for myself, I just know that I could not sleep with another man now until I meet you again. . . . I'll be as faithful as a dutiful and conventional wife just because I could not help it—that is the way it is" (69). A few years later the good wife model still prevails, despite the serious problems the two had already encountered in their transatlantic affair. "Oh Nelson!," Beauvoir writes in 1950, "I'll be so nice and good, you'll see. I'll wash the floor, I'll cook the whole meals, I'll write your book as well as mine, I'll make love to you ten times at night and as much in the day, even if I feel a bit tired" (324). So was Sollers right? It's true that Algren had encouraged Beauvoir to expand her "essay on women" into a book. Deirdre Bair, Beauvoir's biographer, fleshes out the picture: Algren and Beauvoir "had discussed the situation of women when they were in New York in May, sitting and smoking in the twin beds of their hotel room after they made love." Bair notes that Algren "had been fascinated to learn that French women had only just received the vote, and as his questions became more probing they had settled on the topic of 'women's status throughout the world' as [her] possible theme" (353).[8] But if Beauvoir discussed the project that became *The Second Sex* as pillow talk with her lover in New York, Sartre too had played a catalytic (though less orgasmic) role earlier in the story by convincing Beauvoir to write about something he thought she knew about very well—"the condition of women in its broadest terms" (in Bair 325).

The letters shed new light, too, on Beauvoir both as a literary critic and as a reader during the complicated climate of postwar France (she identified herself in public as politically feminist only in the early 1970s). Beauvoir writes to Algren about D. H. Lawrence in November 1948, reporting on her research:

> Among lot of tedious or silly books I am reading about women, I read over Lawrence's novels. It is rather tedious: always the same sex-story, the woman brought to submission by a lover who looks like Lawrence himself, has to kill her own self so they can both be happy. Well, you didn't kill my self and we were pretty happy, were we not? Still, sometimes he speaks with real warmth about love life, of such things in love life nobody dares to speak about; it should be more simple, so it could be moving and good. The beginning of *The Plumed Serpent* is a story of a bull fight in Mexico, but he doesn't feel it the way I did, nor the way you did neither. Tell me if you think anything about Lawrence? (236)

What's striking here is the explicitly autobiographical way Beauvoir describes her critical views on Lawrence. Unlike the forceful but abstract analysis of Lawrence's novels in *The Second Sex*, the letters to Algren reveal a Beauvoir present in the flesh as a physical and sexual being. In the correspondence Beauvoir clearly separates her personal experience with Algren from the ideology that shapes Lawrence's apprehension of sexuality. In other words, she perceives, names, and analyzes in literature what Millett later, without acknowledging the insights of her precursor, would come to call "sexual politics." But unlike Millett, Beauvoir also turned to women writers throughout *The Second Sex* as precious testimony to other views of the female condition.

The ten years that preceded the publication of *Sexual Politics* were, as we might expect from the decade of the sixties, full of sex. But what kind? Or put another way, to what extent did seventies' feminism emerge from reading—or trying to read—literary texts that were banned or newly unbanned in the immediately preceding decades? D. H. Lawrence's 1928 *Lady Chatterley's Lover* was first brought out legally and completely in the United States in 1959 (1960 in England); in 1959 Olympia Press published William Burroughs's *Naked Lunch* in Paris. Like Virginia Woolf, who refers in *A Room of One's Own* to the obscenity trial for Radclyffe Hall's *The Well of Loneliness*, and Sylvia Plath, who writes home to her mother in America about the trial for *Lady Chatterley's Lover* in England, the early feminist critics of sexual politics made literary theory from contemporary readings of male writers famous, not to say infamous, for their views on sex and women: Miller, Lawrence, Kerouac, Mailer, to name the usual suspects (the views were not identical but were not incompatible either). On November 6, 1960, Plath writes that she was lucky enough to have been given a ticket "for the last day of the Lady Chatterley trials at the Old Bailey—very exciting—especially with the surprising verdict of 'not guilty.' So *Penguin Books* can publish the unexpurgated edition—a heartwarming advance for D. H. Lawrence's writings!" (399).[9] Like all politics, literary ones make for odd bedfellows. Lawrence also drew Beauvoir and Millett to his work, though in vastly different modes of appreciation. (If both Lawrence and Miller have had their female fans, as critics and writers, Mailer, Millett's nemesis—who returned the feeling—mainly inspires antipathy.)

Banned books were indeed key to the zeitgeist, and even girls much less downtown than Kate Millett might have dipped into an earlier edition of *Lady Chatterley's Lover,* an underground, pirated copy. My senior year of high school, I note in my diary for 1957, "I read Lady Chatterly's Lover [sic]. I sort of would like a lover. I don't know," I add nervously. I'm excited by the novel but my experience lags sadly behind: "I like it quite a lot. It must be glorious to enjoy sex. I never really have. That one experience with Arthur was so sordid." What happened with Arthur—not to mention, who is Arthur?

How do we live with the books that change our lives, and can you know this—except in retrospect? It would seem impossible to have come to intellectual consciousness between 1957 and 1967 without reading the Beats and hearing about the obscenity trials, though I can't honestly say I remember either from the time. The reading habits of most girls would include the contradictions of high- and lowbrow culture: best-sellers such as Grace Metalious's *Peyton Place* or Herman Wouk's *Marjorie Morningstar,* along with the poetry of T. S. Eliot and Wallace Stevens; Lawrence alongside *True Confessions, Seventeen,* and the *New Yorker.* Plath, herself, was a studious reader of women's magazines and wanted to publish stories in their pages—the "slicks"—for money. These perplexing reading experiences led some girls avid for transgression to try to make their lives resemble the books or at least to look for a different kind of life and world after reading them; for some that meant becoming many years later, though they surely didn't imagine it at the time, feminist critics.

Hettie Jones is one example: "Today," Hettie Jones writes, "I'm sprawled on the bed, thinking about what to do next. I've just finished reading the new, hot book *On the Road.* I love Jack Kerouac's footloose heroes, who've upset complacent America simply by driving through it! . . . I know I don't want to go on the road right now, not while New York is the best place in the world. Nothing could tempt me away" (42). But across the Atlantic, Sheila Rowbotham, restless in the provinces, sets out for Paris from Leeds, inspired by Kerouac and Ginsberg, Burroughs and Mailer published in the *Evergreen Review*, as well as Lawrence unbanned in Penguin. She hoped her reading would help her find what she was seeking, even though, as she puts it in *Promise of a Dream*, Lawrence didn't fit the "dilemmas we faced about how to behave as young women" (10).[10] Rowbotham (two years younger than I) sees her story as part of the sixties.

Fifties or sixties, we were the last generation to get our ideas, if not information about sex from books rather than movies. Miller's *Tropic of Cancer* was published in the United States in 1961, *Capricorn* in 1962. I have a copy of *Cancer* in an Obelisk Press edition published in Paris in 1960. Purchased in Paris (the price is written in francs on the cover), the book serves as the memento of a boy I dated in the spring of 1961, whose name is on the flyleaf. Was this part of his not inconsiderable seduction arsenal, a sexy book to go along with his red MG convertible? In the book approach, he was not alone. In her memoir *Manhattan, When I Was Young*, Mary Cantwell, who came to New York in 1953, describes being introduced to Miller's novel by her husband-to-be: "like everyone who spent his junior year abroad, he came out of Paris with a copy of *Tropic of Cancer* hidden under his train seat. He gave me a copy of *Tropic of Cancer* to read and I tried, really tried, but he may as well have asked me to dash a communion wafer to the floor" (23).[11] I must have tried harder; but I also had less to overcome. If I can still see myself being driven downtown to hear Charlie Mingus and learning to drink Manhattans, I don't remember reading Miller that spring. But I vividly recall my introduction to *Capricorn* in Paris at the suggestion of the man whom I was to marry (he also recommended the work of Georges Bataille—I should have known). In any event, in New York or Paris, barely past virginity and virtually orgasmless at the time, I was floored by Miller's descriptions—mainly of women's sexual appetite.

Sexual Politics opens (how could we forget?) with an excerpt from Henry Miller's novel *Sexus*, set in a bathroom, with the narrator in the bathtub. Ida, the sex partner in question, enters the scene wearing a silk bathrobe and silk stockings. Millett then produces an explication de texte, focusing pedagogically on a crucial detail in the description of the woman as she brings the narrator towels. Here Millett makes an even bolder critical move than starting her book in medium coitum with a woman's pubic hair ("muff") viewed at eye level; she invokes the existence and reaction of a female reader: "The female reader," Millett writes, "may realize that one rarely wears stockings without the assistance of other paraphernalia, girdle or garters, but classic masculine fantasy dictates that nudity's most appropriate exception is some gauze-like material, be it hosiery or underwear" (5).[12] Girdle or garters, ultimately the impact of the passage is not limited to the plausible or implausible detail of undergarments. It's the recognition that reading as a man or a woman might not be the same experience, especially in the face of sexual representation. "What the reader is vicariously experiencing at this juncture is a nearly supernatural sense of power—should the reader be a male. For the passage is not only a vivacious and imaginative use of circumstance, detail, and context to evoke the excitations of sexual intercourse, it is also a male assertion of dominance over a weak, compliant, and rather unintelligent female. It is a case of sexual politics at the fundamental level of copulation. Several satisfactions for the hero and reader alike undoubtedly accrue upon this triumph of the male ego." (6).

And should the reader be not only female but lesbian?

Like Woolf's fictionalized "I" in *A Room of One's Own*, Millett's hypothetical reader is biographically present in the argument. But despite the personal-is-the-political ethos of the late sixties, Millett, again like Woolf in the thirties, was not willing to run the risk of an autobiographical avowal about her own sexual desires in print. The step of imagining an embodied, desiring reader was dangerous enough. During the launch of *Sexual Politics*, moreover,

Millett represented herself as rather publicly married, kissing her husband for the benefit of cameras. Doubtless, the reception history of *Sexual Politics* (like Foucault's later *History of Sexuality*) would have been radically different had personal material entered the author's arguments directly and explicitly, regardless of the fact that those in the know, knew. In *Flying*, Millett's first autobiography (1974), Millett revisits the aftermath of *Sexual Politics*, the pressure on her to confess.[13] Millett recounts her public outing at Columbia in *Flying* with Joycean echoes: "Yes I said yes I am a Lesbian. It was the last strength I had" (15).

In an introduction to the new edition of the autobiography in 1990, Millett describes *Sexual Politics* as a "Ph.D. thesis composed in Mandarin mid-Atlantic to propitiate a committee of professors of English, a colonial situation" (x). This version of history echoes the earlier language of *Flying* where Millett returned in time to the Bowery, to the "red table where I wrote a book, so long ago—writing for professors. Writing when I did not even want to be a writer, just burning with an idea that could make me do a book, call it a thesis, rip off a Ph.D." (43). After the fact of the book for professors, Millett revels in her well-earned autobiographical freedom. "I'd never yet written," Millett admits in the introduction to *Flying*, "in my own voice" (ix).

In 1970 *Sexual Politics* landed Kate Millett on the cover of *Time*, as *Sexual Behavior in the Human Female* had done for Alfred Kinsey in 1953, because she too had hit an exposed nerve in the contemporary culture, a national culture obsessed with sex. This was a moment in American history when ideas about social change and new citizens were shot through with sexual fantasies. *Playboy* published its first issue in 1953. Critics have asked what would have happened if Millett had chosen other literary works through which to ground her claims for sexual politics. Wouldn't she have had to write a different book? Maybe. But that's like saying that Henry Miller would have written the bathtub scene differently if pantyhose had been invented in the 1920s.

Did "bad" sex lead to "good" feminism? Yes and no.

In a conversation published in the *Women's Studies Quarterly* at the beginning of the nineties entitled *"Sexual Politics: Twenty Years Later,"* Kate Millett, Alix Kates Shulman, and Catharine Stimpson reflect on the anniversary of the book and celebrate the publication of a new edition.[14] Millett recalls the historical context of the book's production: "It happened because I got fired. . . . I'd been doing the reading for years; a whole summer for Lawrence. But what I mean is that this became the book it is, even that it became a book at all, taking off with that 'to hell with it' first chapter, rather than another Ph.D. thesis, because at the end of 1968 I was fired from . . . a job [at Barnard College] I would have worked at gladly the rest of my life" (37). (Millett's participation in the Columbia strike eliminated that possibility—given Barnard's institutionally dependent relation on Columbia.) Looking back, Millett emphasizes the collective nature of the thinking that went into the book: "I was the scribe of many" (39). Shulman wishes hopefully that in a postmanifesto era reissue of the book might "provide a certain timely kick" (36). But perhaps the book is too much of its time.

Bad sex, sex driven by male domination, as the phrase went, produced one strand of literary feminism, the one embodied first by Beauvoir then by Millett—the ideological critique of male-authored literature. It was paralleled, of course, by another critically important current in the feminist tide, the resistance to the canonical sexual plot expressed in the work of women reading women's writing—"gynocritics."[15] By the time Plath's novel *The Bell Jar*, published under a pseudonym in England in January 1963, was republished eight years later in the United States, feminism was underway. In the month of April 1971 both *The Bell Jar* and Germaine Greer's *The Female Eunuch* were favorably reviewed in the *New York Times*. Seen through feminist eyes, the doomed girl of the 1950s suddenly made another kind of blinding sense both to reviewers and to readers. Not that the sex was so great, but at least Plath's heroine was, as we said in those days, the subject of desire. However.

IV

A Sentimental Journey

These are the tranquillized *Fifties*,
and I am forty. Ought I to regret my seedtime?
—Robert Lowell, "Memories of West Street
and Lepke"

At the end of "Decades" I resisted the urge to predict the future of feminism, the feminism I had been involved with throughout my academic life. I had begun that meditation when I was looking hard at fifty and thinking fearfully about aging—my own and that of my cohort in feminism. I ended then on an anxious note about no longer wishing to *represent* feminism through my own involvement as a literary critic, turning instead to an autobiographical writing freed from what I took to be that burden and leaving the future of redescribing feminism to new generations. I'm not any more willing now to judge the evolution of second- and third-wave feminism in the nineties.

Rather, as I face down sixty, I'm irresistibly drawn back to the time of youth, to the girl who got conned in 1959. When I examine the girl in my father's snapshot, I read the fifties writ large, a decade in which stories like this happened—me thinking I was on the road when I was still waiting for the prince. I mean Grace Kelly married one, didn't she? A photograph in an October 1959 issue of *Life*, the same number in which the fallen Van Doren prince appears on the cover, features Princess Grace of Monaco engaged in conversation with Charles de Gaulle, her smooth blond hair bound up in a splendid beehive. Conceivably the hairdo could be emulated even with dark hair, but the total picture was a girl's American dream come true.

So what finally is my relation to that girl who sees the world through harlequin glasses? The girl and I both belong to a genealogy that links in an uneasy chain, backward and forward, seventies' feminists to fifties' girls and nineties' professors. I know by the documents that the girl is me, or at least that her pastness is *in* me (the dumbness and unknowing); and when I revisit that time I wish equally to reclaim and disown her. Part of my autobiographical shame is remembering another episode from earlier in the summer of 1959 when I exchanged passionate kisses with a handsome stranger on the ferry from Calais to Dover—another Englishman. Sadly, he was met at the ferry by his beautiful, blonde fiancée. Don't you ever learn, my mother used to sigh with an edge of exasperation. I guess that's the thing about the girl: it took her so long to learn. As always, it's in the private stories behind the public statements, as much as in the collective pronouncements and manifestos, that the history of feminism continues to remain—however embarrassingly—alive. Autobiographical moments provide keys to the emotional logic at work in the culture, and that supplies the juice for any political movement. Stories such as these have a special place in a collective feminist past, for they speak volumes about the brainless furtiveness of prefeminist consciousness.

When I remind myself how thoroughly I was trained, I have more compassion for my younger self and I turn off the critical gaze. I manage to work up some sympathy for her, as I hope you will, if only as exhibit A of this archive. I like myself better as a generic girl true to her time than as "myself." Or rather a certain kind of girl, mostly American but sometimes also English, an adventurous girl on a quest. Reading Sheila Rowbotham's memoir, I discover that in 1961 we might have sat through the same boring Cours de Civilisation at the Sorbonne—French culture packaged for foreigners. Her memories of the crowds of students "spilling out over the pavements of the Boulevard St Michel" (13) send me hunting for a photograph taken that year by the roving photographers who would snap your picture without asking—and sell it to you for a small sum (fig. 3.2). Rowbotham describes unchic English students in duffel coats and there I am in my (American) boyfriend's dark blue duffel coat strolling down the boulevard with a friend. True, not up to the standards of Parisiennes who in winter like spring would wear thin suede jackets, straight skirts, and heels (often without stockings) and not seem to feel the

FIG. 3.2. Me with a French friend, Paris 1961.

cold. But my appearance has improved—with contact lenses and straightened hair.

Still, I can't quite close the gap that separates us whenever I encounter the girl face-to-face; I cringe—or at least wince—when I have to acknowledge our resemblance. But maybe it's time to give her a break. Maybe I can lure her into the more forgiving arms of academic memoir. (After all, I'm not her mother, am I?)

Could I have known that in 1959 Godard would make *Breathless*, a new wave film starring Jean Seberg as a sexy American girl on her own in Paris with a *real* criminal?

Almost forty years later I decided to revisit the scene of the crime. I took the train from London and stopped at Oxford on my way to Stratford, looking for clues. I'm doing research, I would say when asked, on the fifties. Victoria, my student, who was writing a dissertation on gender and architecture, studying floor plans and blueprints, accompanied me. My memory work dragged her out of the library, but at least she got to see Stratford and Oxford, where she'd never been. I was spending a sabbatical year in Paris, and she was in London on a grant; it was a piece of luck that we were able to make this journey into lost time together.

When we arrived at Stratford (we stopped at Oxford on the way back), we went directly to the police station. I wanted to see the record of my experience, maybe even the face of my con man again. The police were polite but discouraging, and permission to see the files, if files from 1959 there were, would have to be pursued by the mail. The visit to the Shakespeare Institute was equally fruitless. The records had been transferred to the University of Birmingham since that summer program was now defunct; the secretaries at the institute gave me a name and an address. The last stop was the theater. We sat through a numbingly long modern dress performance of *Macbeth* at the Royal Shakespeare Theatre in the company of solemn schoolchildren. Afterward, the two of us braved the clouds of smoke at The Dirty Duck and watched the actors come in, drink, unwind, flirt.

We stayed the night, still hoping for a piece of involuntary memory to bubble up from the dirty waters of the Avon. From Paris I had asked Victoria to try and book rooms at the Barwyn, the bed and breakfast our group of students had lived in during the summer of 1959. No one at the booking agency had heard of the Barwyn, and the only room she could find was a wildly overpriced one at the Grovesnor House. When we checked out of the hotel, we inquired at the desk whether anyone knew what had happened to the Barwyn, only to learn that twenty years earlier, three hotels that had stood side-by-side—one of them the Barwyn—had been bought up and incorporated into a single entity. The Barwyn had vanished as a separate establishment, but its previous existence was marked within Grovesnor House by a meeting room dubbed "The Barwyn Room," a refashioned trace of its former self. Without knowing it, Victoria and I had spent the night with the ghosts of the Barwyn's old walls. Victoria took photographs of me standing in front of the hotel, pointing at the garden beds remembered from a slide my parents had taken that fateful summer (from a visit I do not remember). But what about the ghost of my former self?

In February 1997 I received two letters in response to my Stratford inquiries. The first from the Warwickshire Constabulary reads in part, "Unfortunately police records relating to that time and indeed up to more recent years, have all been destroyed as policy and procedure dictates. I can find no trace of X [I had given him the name Judy had recorded in her diary] and therefore must assume that the professional con man may also have used an alias. It is with regret that I am unable to assist you further with your memoirs however may I take this opportunity of wishing you well in your venture." This letter is signed by a man appointed to the CRIME DESK, as he styled his function. The second arrived on my fifty-sixth birthday (a birthday I could hardly have fathomed then); it, too, closed the door on further evidential research. "Unfortunately because of storage space we do not keep records for so long: I have checked through the publicity leaflet for that year, but there is nothing there for the Stratford summer school. . . . We are sorry that we are unable to be of any help, but wish you good luck with the memoir." Both letters promptly answered my request for information; both correspondents courteously assured me that they found my project interesting. I still haven't written the memoir I had announced in my letter of inquiry, but somehow converting the con man fiasco into an artifact of fifties' culture has provided a small reward.[16] If I started out too late to find the truth, at least I've recovered a piece of lost time. And for me, memory trumps history every time.

Did I ever learn? I'm not sure, but Reader, I didn't marry him— the con or the boyfriend. And yes, I've finally given up on the prince.

A while ago, I ran into a former student, wise beyond her years. We sat down for an espresso at a counter in a coffee shop on Broadway (before Starbucks made this a commonplace possibility)—not quite a Parisian café but a lot better than drinking permanently reheated, percolated coffee in a greasy spoon (like Tom's, the restaurant frequented by *Seinfeld* characters, and the local hangout of my graduate student days at Columbia). "So how are you?" I recited the litany of dissatisfactions, all the things that hadn't happened, and now never would. The child, the really good job. She listened, familiar with my shtick, and then said: "Didn't some things happen that you *hadn't* expected?" Caught short by the turn, I had to consider the point. So why didn't those things count; why couldn't I see that for some people they might also weigh in the balance. Beyond the hopeless calculus of my unconscious (in which other people have what I want and I, to my eternal disappointment, have nothing), I finally said that I hadn't started out wanting what I had since learned to take for granted; that because I had never dreamed about a career (one of the things) the way I had dreamed, say, about the prince, whatever it might mean, it wasn't the realization of an adolescent fantasy. But I had to admit that if what I had was not a dream come true, it was true nevertheless.

4

The Marks of Time

Q. How do you feel about growing older?
A. Any woman who says she doesn't care about aging is lying.

—Interview with Catherine Deneuve in
Elle, November, 1995

I loathe my appearance now: the eyebrows slipping down towards the eyes, the bags underneath, the excessive fullness of the cheeks, and that air of sadness around the mouth that wrinkles always bring.

—Simone de Beauvoir, *Force of Circumstance*

I

Mirror, Mirror

What does a woman of a certain age see when she looks at herself in time's mirror?

Four faces, four bronze autoportraits by sculptor Sheila Solomon (fig. 4.1). They belong to an installation called *Time/ Pieces*: nineteen sculptures and two drawings that engage with the questions of women, change, and time. Solomon conceived the work as an "organic whole with the pieces resonating and amplifying one another. . . . The organization of the works is circular," she writes, "in that it reaches back into my past and extends forward into the future."[1] Between the portrait covered with hands

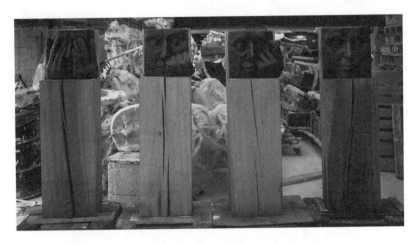

FIG. 4.1. The four autoportraits.
Courtesy of the artist. Photo shot in the foundry. An-My Lê. All photographs of Solomon's unless noted otherwise are by An-My Lê.

and the uncovered one exists the task of face work: dealing with one's face as it changes over time. Solomon's heads and figures embody the vision of a woman who looked at herself head on— and from all angles—in midlife for more than a decade. When I first saw these pieces, I caught my breath and thought: this is a woman not afraid of the mirror. As Solomon said later in response to one of my questions: "my body has been good to me." How we interpret the bodiliness of aging is intimately bound up with the story of seeing ourselves as women in the first place. "I don't think I know a single woman," Barbara Grizzuti Harrison writes in *An Accidental Autobiography*, "who knows what she looks like" (16).[2] Through *Time/Pieces* I've come to think about aging as a project as well as a process of coming to terms with a changing face and body, an oscillation between the mirrored poles of acceptance and refusal.

II

Reflections

In an essay devoted to her friend the writer Alfred Chester, Cynthia Ozick meditates on time's betrayal: "Passing my reflection in a shopwindow," Ozick writes, "I am taken by surprise at the sight of a striding woman with white hair: she is still wearing the bangs of her late youth, but there are shocking pockets and trenches in her face; she has a preposterous dewlap; she is no one I can recognize."[3] In this portrait of a writer (a contemporary) as a minor literary light—a coming-of-age story set in postwar New York—Ozick never returns to the question of her own face in the shopwindow. The experience of mistaking herself for another (who *is* that woman looking back at me in the mirror?), someone other than herself—"a woman with white hair" and a "preposterous dewlap"—seems to interest Ozick only metaphorically, as an example of how we can be surprised by time. She calls this discrepancy a "generational pang": the realization that the minds that currently interest her belonged to "little children" when she was learning—precociously—to think and write (79).

In *Aging and Its Discontents* Kathleen Woodward comments on Freud's "shock of recognition" upon encountering his elderly double in the mirror, a "dismaying" experience that he recounts in a note to the essay "The Uncanny." What Freud sees, Woodward argues, is "the image of the Other, to use Beauvoir's terminology, an image Freud would prefer not to recognize" (65).[4] Following Woodward's rereading of Freud, we can wonder whether the way Ozick dismisses the shock of coming up against her face in the mirror, the alacrity with which the writer immediately moves on to questions of memory, might not also be a form of repression that leaves intact the belief that in her unconscious—like Freud's— she is forever young. Ozick goes on instead to delineate different models of biographical identity. She wants to evoke "certain exactnesses," neither "memoir" (a genre dismissed as "that souvenir elevation of trifles") nor a "fixity of self" but, rather, what she will call "platonic enclosures or islands"—something like "clear photographs"—a form of memory "independent of time, though not of place" (79). It's one of those islands of intensity that allows her to remember in print (in a form that strangely resembles that of the memoir) the writer Alfred Chester as he was—when he was young—and she was, too.

III

Looking One's Age

There's a color photograph that captures the style of emotional entanglement between my mother and me in the mid-sixties (fig. 4.2). My mother is about the age I am now as I write. In the photograph, two women look at each other across their war. We are alone, fixed in our struggle. My father loved this picture which he had enlarged from a color slide and framed. It hung in the dinette and presided over meals. It's a good picture, he said.

Not long after my mother's death my sister and I began fighting over

FIG. 4.2. My mother and me circa 1965.
Photograph by my father, Louis Kipnis.

the best way for my father to lead his new life alone. (The building was going co-op, and he needed to decide whether to buy the rent-controlled apartment he'd lived in for fifty years.) My sister turned on me and said bitterly: "You're just like Mommy, you'd kill to get what you want." I'd never thought I was anything like my mother—I identified against her, with my father—but maybe my sister was right. I can see how I have become my mother. It's not so easy to know who you are like—and sometimes this resemblance changes over time.

Going through my mother's clothes after her death, I found in the pockets of every coat (and she had many, many coats) the traces of her commitment to personal comfort: a crumpled-up kleenex and a wrapped coffee candy. I was struck by the regularity with which these items turned up. Recently, taking some of my (many) coats to the cleaners, I emptied out the pockets and I found in each a crumpled up-kleenex (the same leaky nose) and a box of Ricola mints (the same need to have something in our mouth).

My mother lives in my pockets and also in my face. In the mirror, I silently measure with her the spreading pores, the advancing crepe, lines that crease even earlobes. I think: In fifteen years I, too, could be dead. Of course that doesn't tell me what I need to know. How to live with this face—our face—in the face of death. How to live without that other against whom we think we know who we are.[5]

In the *Elle* interview from which I've drawn my epigraph to this chapter, Catherine Deneuve responds to a question about cosmetic surgery: "By the number of surgeons in Paris who claim to have operated on me, I should look like the bride of Frankenstein. That said, I find it wonderful to slow down the marks of time—so long as the face matches the rest of the body. You have to look at yourself objectively."[6] What does it mean to have your face match the rest of your body? Should you have your body fixed to match your face? Or is it the other way round? Above all, what would it mean to look at yourself objectively? "How is it possible to look at our bodies objectively," Harrison asks, "(and with love)?" (31).

Deneuve's understanding of objectivity is at war with her commitment to delaying the visible signs of the aging process. To an earlier question about turning fifty, and whether she would lie about her age, Deneuve responds: "I never hide my age—it's a question of pride. I'm often struck when people say, 'You're so youthful!'—as if they saw me as an image, not a human being. There are people who don't seem to realize I've been around for quite a while. They must have some idea of my age, but maybe my face doesn't correspond with their notion of what a fifty-year-old woman looks like." What does fifty look like? People who think that they know what fifty looks like—old, unattractive, a face bearing the marks of time—are surprised by Deneuve's "youthful" face. But Deneuve's face, in which the marks of time have been "slowed down," maybe even erased, is not a face in which "fifty" has been allowed to appear. Again, what is "fifty"? Like the famous Steinem remark around the event of her fiftieth birthday—"This is what fifty looks like"—fifty exists in the eye of the beholder. In her biography of Steinem, *The Education of a Woman*, Carolyn Heilbrun notes that Steinem was in fact repeating the quip first uttered when she turned forty, adding at fifty, the less frequently quoted words: "We've been lying for so long, who would know" (355).[7] In another interview from that year, Deneuve answers the question about plastic surgery and lying about age a little differently: "Of course I've had some face work," she admits.[8] She says this so that "other women won't feel demoralized." You say you've had face work so that other women won't feel so bad about looking the way they look. With a little face work, you too could look like Catherine Deneuve. At sixty, Steinem at least had the grace to not say this is what sixty looks like (great, let me tell you, viewed from across a seminar table); the only face work involved, Steinem admits in "Bodies of Knowledge," was having some fat removed from her eyelids so that she could "wear sleep-in contact lenses" and see "the ceiling when I look up at it from my bed in the morning and my feet when I look down in the shower" (241).

The two streaked blonde icons—feminine and feminist (though Steinem's appearance is also "feminine") are and aren't talking about the same thing. Aging—in public, visually. In an interview for the *New York Times*, Deneuve talks about the "marks" left by the "passage of the years" and what this means for a movie star: "It's a very visual profession, even if one's career is not based on looks. Cinema is still something people first see and then hear. Beauty is not everything, but it still has a power of attraction" (8). I doubt very much that Deneuve enjoys the arrival of age spots on her hands and celebrates their presence, the way Steinem says she does, as the friendly proof of the wonderful experiences she's had over a lifetime. "I ask them what they have to say for themselves. 'A banner held in liver-spotted hands' " (257).[9] Still, both famously gorgeous women point to the same question for the rest of us mere female mortals: How do you know what you look like over time? How does time produce its own scrim of interpretation? It's hard to resist the narrative of decline, especially when the public faces of female icons—Deneuve, Jackie O, like all media-produced images—are carefully adjusted *not to age* over time. Deneuve's face (and before her, Brigitte Bardot's) appeared on the standard-issue postage stamp as the face to the figure "Marianne" (who embodies the French republic) during the 1990s—the perfection of her face fixed in public memory.

Resistance requires an active, arduous engagement with the general cultural assumption that as women we are at our most beautiful or desirable at a youthful moment and the rest is downhill. Here is a photograph of me at twenty-eight, which represents my interpretation of what Ozick may mean by "platonic enclosures"; the photograph was taken at a turning point, a liminal place in my life—my decision, post-1968, to go to graduate school and the brief fantasy of making my life with an artist, a man I loved and admired, who went on to become a famous sculptor. My father had the photo framed (fig. 4.3). After my father's death, I brought the photograph home and set it on a sideboard (vintage sixties teak that also came from my parents' apartment) in my study. When students come to see me at home, they unfailingly comment on the picture. "That's you?" they ask, hesitating on the threshold of disbelief. "Yes," I say lightly, "that's me when I was young and gorgeous." Then, evading the invitation to flattery, they say, "you still have that look"—the warning in my eyes that

FIG. 4.3. Me post-1968.
Photograph by Martin Puryear.

says, "cross me at your peril." They've told me that they fear the look that summarizes what one of my students called in the acknowledgments to her dissertation, "my impossibly high standards" (on the other hand, how scared could they be if they *tell* me about it?). Sometimes, too, I think that they are comforted by the contrast between then and now. However unselfconsciously, they know that they are *young* women—many of them beautiful and sexy as well as smart—and enjoying their beauty, now. At the same time, I also know that their looks don't mean as much to *them* as they do to me; just as I take my books for granted while theirs are still before them. When I was twenty-eight, of course, I didn't think I was young and gorgeous . . . I was just twenty-eight and worrying whether I would ever be happy. Books were nowhere visible on my horizon of expectations. The photograph is how I feel myself to be when I'm not looking in the mirror; it represents a kind of double forgetfulness, both about my appearance and about all that has happened since then. Recently I moved the photograph to a top shelf in my bookcase to displace the evidence of that discrepancy—and the reminder it never fails to bring me of the island's remoteness.

At the end of her sixties Carolyn Heilbrun offers a meditation on the meaning of women's aging inspired by her discussion of Steinem's fiftieth birthday:

> Turning fifty, both in anticipation and actuality, is a watershed in a woman's life. . . . First comes despair at the aging body, and particularly the aging face, a despair whose alleviation can be sought either by impersonating youth with the aid of drugs, surgery, or makeup, or by abandoning all hope of a youthful appearance and accepting with wry humor the inevitable expanding and sagging. . . . Only recently and gradually has the possibility emerged in female consciousness that something might be gained for women at the cusp of fifty. . . . For the woman turning fifty . . . the reconsideration that surrounds that moment may and often does provide sufficient impetus profoundly to reenvision her life. (355–56)

The body, the face. The eyes, the breast. Vulnerable zones for women aging. The breast shows the marks of time but, more important, becomes—randomly, rampantly—the target of cancer for many women. There's an odd way, as we'll see, in which breast cancer arrives as a crucial part of the aging process for too many women. (Sometimes, of course, it marks the end of the process altogether.) In part as an effect of breast cancer, in part as an effect of therapy, in her early fifties Steinem set out to reenvision her life; it all entailed "looking within." Though reviewers found Steinem's discovery of her interiority naive or sentimental (her "inner child"), we might more generously understand the trope of turning inward, "looking within," as a way of turning away from the mirror—maybe putting your hands over your face—from tracking the damage to that face long enough to think about, say, how it is that we came to think we knew what our face—or body—was.

IV

Body Parts

How does any woman know what she looks like? How does she learn to recognize what she looks like—from the outside? The look of the look in the mirror. She begins, for most of us, as Adrienne Rich (after Beauvoir) has famously argued in *Of Woman Born*, by observing her mother whom she examines by body parts, as though in childhood she had intuited the anatomy of female destiny.[10]

I saw my own mother's menstrual blood before I saw my own. Hers was the first female body I ever looked at, to know what women were, what I was to be. I remember taking baths with her in the hot summers of early childhood, playing with her in the cool water. As a young child I thought how beautiful she was; a print of Botticelli's Venus on the wall, half-smiling, hair flowing, associated itself in my mind with her.

In early adolescence I still glanced slyly at my mother's body, vaguely imagining: I too shall have breasts, full hips, hair between my thighs—whatever that meant to me then, and with all the ambivalence of such a thought. And there were other thoughts: I too shall marry, have children—but *not like her*. I shall find a way of doing it all differently.   (219)

There was no getting away from my mother's body. After a bath, she would emerge clothed simply in a towel: a white towel tied around her waist. She would often lie on top of the bed in the towel and read or work the crossword puzzle. When my sister and I were little, we would walk in on her during her bath; even much later, we would come barging in (her word) with a request, since in the tub she was almost always in a good mood. Later, I remember thinking that her body resembled our saddle shoes, two-toned: tanned, freckled arms and legs from playing tennis, pale torso and white, pear-shaped breasts, erect, darkish pink nipples. The body I remember is not the half-submerged body of my childhood memories, though; it is the mother's body seen from my adolescence, the body I saw at twelve and thirteen as I waited for my own body to reveal its secrets.

"Did your breasts always sag like that?" This is not a question I ever admitted asking, though I'm sure it was on my lips as I stared down at my mother's stretched-out form, studying her body. Years later my mother, still walking through the apartment with a towel tied around her waist, would tell that story laughing, as proof of what she had to endure from her hostile daughter, but also with the confidence of a woman proud of her breasts. If I ever grew breasts, what—or whose—would they be like? Both grandmothers were all bosom. Their breasts filled their entire chest (a "C" at least, if not a "D"). My mother edged up to a "B." My sister and I barely made it to an "A." Where did the breasts go? The alphabet in reverse in three generations.

Sometimes it seems as if there is only one body: hers unchanging from age twenty-eight—when she is my new mother—to sixty-eight when she began to die. Her hair has gone from black (blue black, she liked to say) to silver, but the body kept its form and style. How can that be?

How do you know what you look like as a woman? It's not so much about what you look like as how you interpret what you see.

I turn now to the work of some contemporary women artists and photographers, who, like Solomon, have begun to change the inherited gaze of female beauty.

In an interview about her show at the Horodner Romley Gallery (1993), Mira Schor talks about the history behind a series of paintings in which she used punctuation marks to visualize the boundaries between public and private experience.[11] In one she wrote out P U B (L) I C to evoke the pubic/public boundary so prominent in the Anita Hill/Clarence Thomas affair. "That led," Schor explains,

> to painting incarnated punctuation marks: cunts, breasts, and penises framed by quote marks; red commas and semicolons set into pubic hair, embedded in flesh. Gender positions, no matter how gory their physicality, are put into question by the quotation marks. Markers of printed language are sexualized, and text, which had been so dominant over visuality in feminist theory and art in the 80s, is presented for its visual seductivity and bodily contingency.

What does it mean to put your breasts into quotation marks? See them as "gender positions," of which *Implant* is only a literal example? (fig. 4.4). I was bemused, if not gratified, by Schor's *"Breast"*— the fact that this particular style of breasts gets named generically *"Breast"*—not least because mine resemble the painting (fig. 4.5). Looking at breasts—and recognizing the perception of their shape and destiny as not so much natural, or even personal, as political— leads Schor to a particular brand of feminist wit (*Against Gravity*, fig. 4.6).

Many years ago, I had an affair with a Frenchman (an art historian, no less) who described my breasts as *"deux oeufs sur le plat."* The French way of saying flat as a pancake, or literally, two eggs sunny-side up. At the time, I thought that was unfair since his language flattened out what were also two nice if little . . . mounds. But I confess that when I saw Mira's painting I thought, well, maybe he had a point.

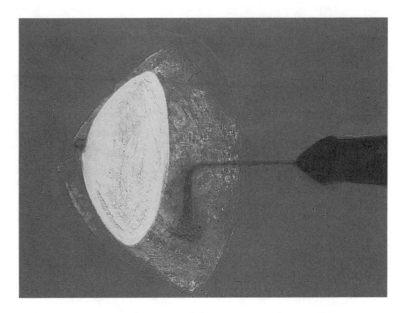

FIG. 4.4. *Implant*, 1992. Oil on canvas. 12 in. x 16 in.

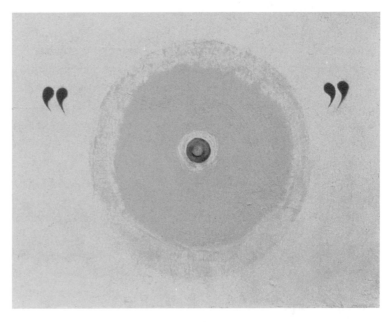

FIG. 4.5. *"Breast,"* 1993. Oil on linen. 12 in. x 16 in. *Private collection.*

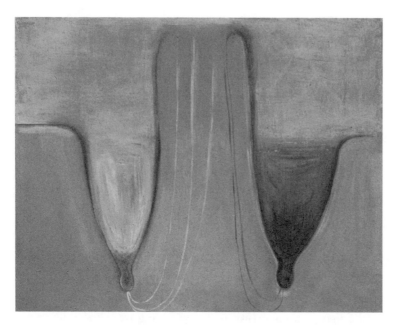

FIG. 4.6. *Against Gravity*, 1989. Oil on canvas. 16 in. x 20 in.
Courtesy of the artist.

One day last winter I walked into the locker room at my gym and saw a large naked woman with huge breasts—watermelons, to stick with the food metaphors, fruits as measurements for breasts and tumors. She had been powdering herself, I guess, or putting lotion on, and was flipping her breasts (sort of like pizza dough) to dry them. I stood there mesmerized thinking about what it would mean to have breasts like that. What happens to my identification with women when I look at those breasts—in action? Were we even in the same story?

If learning to see oneself—as a woman—aging can't be separated from how we've learned to see ourselves as women in the first place, part of how to find new ways of perceiving ourselves as aging bodies and faces is to construct a narrative in which these images can be read, otherwise.

One of the boldest explorers of this territory is British photographer Jo Spence. In her posthumously published book *Cultural Sniping*—a collection of essays dating from the mid-seventies to the early nineties—Spence defines her undertaking as an autobiographical project in which she tried to tell—in images—the story of who she was and how she came to rethink both her work and her place in it.[12] "As soon as I knew I was telling myself a story that made sense to me I felt I had discovered a major structuring absence," Spence writes, "a frame in the middle of my identity. There are no categories for artists who invoke notions of class. . . . Now . . . I see that I am no longer an ugly duckling trying to be a swan but that I belong to a very specific and previously unlabeled group" (161–63). The radical change of view came from the sensation of having a "body in crisis"; as part of her refusal to be victimized by the disease, Spence decided to document through photographs her reactions to breast cancer and the "shame" of ugliness, of feeling that she had a "deformed and injured body" (158).

The series "Narratives of Dis-Ease" was produced in collaboration with a cancer doctor, Tim Sheard, who wanted to understand Spence's experience in the hospital as a patient. Spence makes explicit the bridge from the work she did on her own life-and-death struggle with cancer to the question of aging women's bodies. "The results were very painful, particularly those prints which showed the ways in which my body is not only badly scarred and damaged, but also ageing, overweight and deteriorating" (fig. 4.7). ("I . . . opened the gown and wrote 'monster' across my chest, because that's how I experienced myself as a cancer patient: monstrous to other people" [211]). In displaying these self-portraits of "an ageing/older woman," Spence wants her images to be understood as "an act of solidarity" with other women caught in this collective dilemma (140). The experiments in self-display include masks created in a workshop whose aim is to produce identifications with "certain structures of feelings and experience"—with her grandmother's life, for instance (178). The mask used in the imaginary self-portrait "Crone" offers an unsettling preview of aging (perhaps) to come (fig. 4.8).

If literal masks give us different faces, making it possible to project ourselves into other bodies in time and space, faces are also social masks that we put on or peel off—a layering of selves, no single one more authentic than the other, metaphors of identity—part of what Spence often calls the "masquerade" (161). In her memoir *Autobiography of a Face,* Lucy Grealy describes the denouement of the story she tells of a girl who grows up with part of her face missing through the effects of cancer.[13] After the many operations to arrive at the semblance of a "normal" face, she finds herself surprised by effects of her transformation: "As a child I had expected my liberation to come from getting a new face to put on, but now I saw it came from shedding something, shedding my image" (222). Grealy imagines shedding the ugly self, lifting up the skin, and pulling it back to make a new image. This sounds a lot like the process of the facelift. But a new face—the lifting of the old—like the treatment of breast cancer requires a literal cut. What will win out, the figure or the knife?

Ill with leukemia, as well as with the recurrence of breast cancer, Spence continued to keep "a visual diary about the crisis of representation that I'm passing through" (217). But the last image of *Cultural Sniping,* an untitled photograph, was taken by Spence's

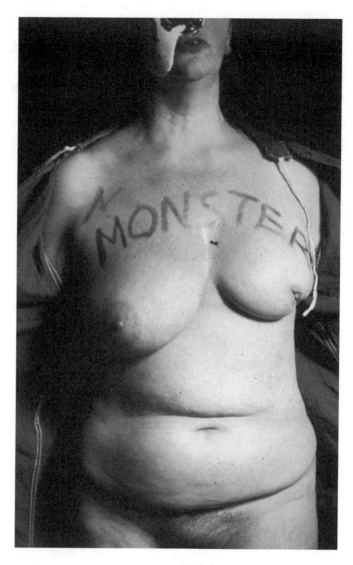

FIG. 4.7. *Exiled.*
Jo Spence/Dr. Tim Sheard, undated.

FIG. 4.8. *Crone.*
Jo Spence / Dr. Tim Sheard.

collaborator, Terry Dennett (227) (fig. 4.9). Jo Spence died at the age of fifty-eight. Until the very end, this was a body committed to work, a working body—and a woman determined to look at her face straight on. Looking at us and urging us to look, too. To look beyond the mask.

And yet, charmingly, I think, despite her commitment to undermining the ideologies of youthful beauty, Spence struggled as many of us (I certainly) do, with the siren call of convention.

> Now that I am moving on to work on ageing, the breast has taken on a completely different set of meanings for me. Last year I had a tragic love affair with a bloke (tragic in that it didn't work out). I was rejected because of my age, because I don't look "beautiful." He didn't want this clapped-out working-class woman who has a spirit and an intellect but also a badly scarred breast and is overweight. These other structuring presences of male desire are there, however much you love and respect your body or your class background for having got you to this stage in your life. I still would like to look like a 25-year-old. I feel a bit daft even saying it.   (211)

By the time Spence died, she was as thin as the bloke might have wanted her to be.

Although she was never really fat, my mother had weighed more than she wanted to. After two months of not eating, she had at last melted into the size she longed to be. Despite its obvious frailty, her newly slim body was unnervingly youthful. And her face revealed the bone structure she had always maintained was the source of true beauty. My mother was particularly gratified by the confession of a friend's husband (a doctor who happened to see patients in the hospital where she had her chemo) that he hadn't realized how beautiful she was—until she was dying. So I guess you could say that my mother died finally looking the way she had wished to live: beautiful and thin.

I want to juxtapose Spence's autobiographical documents with a roughly contemporary picture that caused a sensation when it appeared on the cover of the August 15, 1993, Sunday *New York*

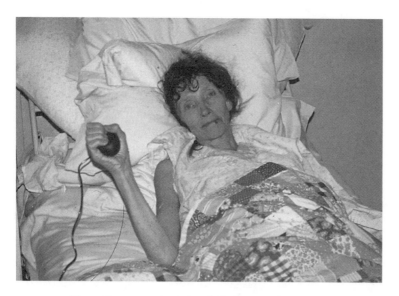

FIG. 4.9. Terry Dennett, 1992. Untitled. Jo Spence on a "good day" shortly before her death, photographing visitors to her room at the Marie Curie Hospice, Hampstead.

Times Magazine (fig. 4.10). This self-portrait of a strikingly beautiful woman, Matuschka, artist, photographer, and model, presents
another—and equally disturbing—way both to challenge the
acceptable limits of female self-representation and to expose the
effects of breast cancer surgery. It was also selected to launch the
New York Times 100th Anniversary issue's narrative of the nineties, a
decade in which women became highly visible advocates for breast
cancer awareness. The glamor and drama of the image "drew
worldwide attention and won the photographer numerous awards"
(158);[14] it helped draw attention to the politics of treatment.
Matuschka's breast was removed after she developed cancer in
1991. In 1999 JoAnne Motichka (the artist known as Matuschka)
successfully sued her doctor "for past and future pain and suffering." The jury granted her $2.2 million, confirming her claim that
the doctor had misread her pathology report and performed an
unnecessary mastectomy (43).[15] The doctor's lawyers appealed
twice and lost, but they succeeded in having the award substantially
reduced. When their request for a third and final appeal was denied
in January 2002, Matuschka was awarded $1,050,000.

IV

"Mother End"

> Brave Orchid rushed along beside her reflection in the
> glass. She used to be young and fast; she was still fast and
> felt young. It was mirrors, not aches and pains that turned
> a person old, everywhere white hair and wrinkles. Young
> people felt pain.
> —Maxine Hong Kingston, *The Woman Warrior*

My mother used to say with a kind of bewilderment about the
person she had become, "Inside I'm still sixteen," incredulous that
she had actually become a woman old enough (though it was
already not in the cards) to be a grandmother: a woman in her six-

FIG. 4.10. Matuschka, self-portrait, August 15, 1993.

ties. In her eyes the two of them, girl and woman, existed on a long continuum of habit and emotion. When I was sixteen and scrutinizing my mother's body for clues about life to come as a woman, I failed to see the connection: "She says that I stare at her," I wrote in my diary, "and that my ideas of old age are stupid and horrible." The old age of a woman in her forties; the panic of a girl who reads disaster in that future. Oh no, not me. But I've begun to understand her feeling about the paradoxical timelessness of age in a new way: my twenty-eight is her sixteen, locations of the past that in retrospect we've idealized—the perfect Platonic form of our liminal selves. And now I've joined her sixties.

What has to happen for a younger woman to identify with an older one? "I am beginning to reach the age," Annie Ernaux writes in her diary *Exteriors* as she approaches fifty, "when I say hello to the old women I meet in my neighborhood, anticipating the moment in life when I shall be one of them. When I was twenty I didn't notice them; they would be dead before my face had wrinkles" (73).[16] Turning fifty is to begin to reimagine not only life after wrinkles—one's own and the lives of others—but life *with* them (wrinkles and other women).

When absorbed in what I'm doing, I forget who and where I am; if I turn and suddenly catch myself in the mirror, I often have the shock of misrecognition Ozick describes. That matron walking down Broadway is my mother but it's also *me*. When did I become her? When did I stop being twenty-eight? The story of how one gets there is the story Jo Spence wanted to understand. Sheila Solomon, to come back full circle now, tells that story, too. *Time/Pieces* begins with a self-portrait of a woman with her arms folded under her breasts, and across her slightly rounded belly are etched the words "Mother End" (fig. 4.11). A woman's life after reproduction.

Toward the end of her series appear "The Guardians." The three eight-foot-tall figures, modeled on Solomon's body and three times its size, are bolted to wood—rough-hewn poplar. They are meant to evoke Roman road markers, herms—classical male figures representing Hermes, which served as public signposts, some-

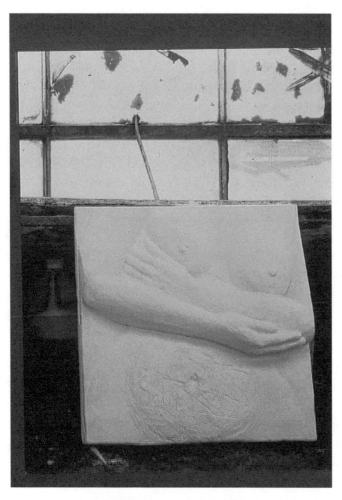

FIG. 4.11. Sheila Solomon. *Mother End*. Plaster.
Courtesy of the artist.

times also grave markers. "The Guardians" divide space and provide a sense of boundary, where you enter and exit. They are associated with the idea of journey—personal and mythical. You see them at a crossroads. The figures are identical, but to the viewer they seem to be different. The eyes are focused and looking. They see you, even if they don't meet your gaze, reflect you.

One winter day I went to have a look at the Guardians. I also thought I might try and have my picture taken in the garden outside Sheila's studio to get a sense of scale. I walked over to the middle Guardian to have a closer look and found myself irresistibly leaning into it (fig. 4.12). When Sheila saw the picture, we both realized immediately that this shot would be the mark of our collaboration. I like the idea of leaning into, resting against this large impassive female body, so unafraid of the world, so sublimely indifferent to the passage of time, but marking it nonetheless. I've found myself thinking that this is what we need as we age: the figure of an older female body occupying time and space—a public figure, though, not an intimate one. The comfort of another form of recognition, outside the family. I see myself in relation to her, and she is not me.

I would be lying, as Deneuve declared, if I said I don't care about growing older, that I prefer this picture of me outside the studio to my indoor sullen, stony portrait at twenty-eight. But perhaps in time I'll take my hands away from my face and see what's out there to lean on. Other selves like us and different, who've also journeyed in time. That might feel less lonely.

As I was writing this piece, I was also getting ready to have a picture taken for my new book. A first set of poses by a young cousin who was a budding photographer failed for technical reasons (though it's also true that the one salvageable print was hardly flattering). So I decided to hire a professional photographer, since my editor had put this in the budget. On the photographer's advice (but I didn't need much persuading) I decided to have professional makeup done. The two women conferred. The eyes are the first to go, the makeup woman explained. I put myself in her hands. When

FIG. 4.12. Me, leaning against one of the Guardians.
Photograph by Sandy Petrey.

the contact sheet came, I was incredibly nervous. I tore open the envelope and took out a magnifying glass. Oh, God, it's not me. (Joan Collins minus the boobs.) True, I looked good (I had eyes), but too good—too much bad stuff had been erased—circles, pouches, droop (fig. 4.13). Imagining friends and colleagues seeing my remade face on the cover, I thought, people will never recognize me. And then I thought, no, it doesn't matter, it's not ... "me." It's only my author-photo mask, no more "real" than the face of disaster in my cousin's shots of me, sitting in the park with natural light, or the face I take to work.

But finally the photo I chose from the contact sheet of possibilities was a face closer to (but still much better than) my own. A face that through makeup showed only faint traces of the marks of time. This shot was taken in Tribeca on the photographer's roof. Invisible in the picture but there in the background is the glorious Woolworth building where at the close of his career my father had rented office space. It felt right that this picture should appear on the jacket of a book largely inspired by his death.

<hr/>

But they are young, these people who suddenly find that they are old. One day I said to myself: "I'm forty!" By the time I recovered from the shock of that discovery I had reached fifty. The stupor that seized me then has not left me yet. I can't get around to believing it.

—Simone de Beauvoir, *Force of Circumstance II*

Simone de Beauvoir was fifty-one years old when she drew the map of catastrophe her face had become in her eyes; fifty-one when she recorded the shock she experienced in moving into another decade. Her biographer Deirdre Bair observes that the photographs from that time do not reflect the face Beauvoir saw in the mirror; rather they "show a woman whose physical appearance is the exact opposite. Her skin is taut, her face unlined; no bags, no wrinkles" (541).[17] Beauvoir recognizes that what she sees as the horror of her appearance derives from the chronology that

FIG. 4.13. Author photo. Makeup by Fern Feller.
Photograph by Kristine Larsen.

inhabits her mind and gaze—not the view of others. She remembers thinking that at forty, "old age is watching and waiting for me." Now it's happened. Before, Beauvoir remembers, she could "look at [her] face without displeasure." She gave it no thought; "it could look after itself." No longer. Still, this is not a matter of what the camera sees—or others. "Perhaps the people I pass in the street see merely a woman in her fifties who simply looks her age, no more, no less. But when I look, I see my face as it was, attacked by the pox of time for which there is no cure" (378).[18] The problem of the cure lies in the nature of the gaze, not time. Bair speculates that Beauvoir's anguish about her physical appearance translated an obsessional fear of death—not her own mortality so much as Sartre's or, rather, the fear of losing him that she equated with total loss, the end of the world. Beauvoir worked through the panic, a fear of death that had gripped her for most of her life, fell in love again, radically changed her life, and became more rather than less engaged in public life. But despite her success in keeping this terror at bay by hard work, writing, politics (and love), I think it's worth noting the obvious (and selfishly, to my mind, comforting) fact that even Simone de Beauvoir was not exempt from the cruelty of the mirror scene that staggers so many women in middle age, in their fifties. Still, I don't want to make too much of this self-portrait of a woman distraught about her looks since it will all add up rather differently in subsequent chapters of her life and autobiography. "The first thing that strikes me," she writes in the next volume, *All Said and Done*, "when I look back at the ten years that have passed since I finished *Force of Circumstance* is that I do not feel that I have aged. Between 1958 and 1962 [Beauvoir turned fifty in 1958] I was aware that I had crossed a frontier. Now that frontier lies behind me, and I have resigned myself to it" (38).[19] The metaphor of crossing a line is very close in structure to what Heilbrun described (looking at Steinem and other women at that moment in their lives) as a watershed, a turning point that opens onto another horizon of possibility beyond the mirror but radically different in spirit at the time of the experience. To cross that frontier is also to relinquish the habits of a certain language, a concern that impedes the journey like excess baggage. Looking back, that shedding can seem an opportunity for change; in the moment it may feel more like the end of the line.

Rereading Beauvoir now at sixty has brought me up short. I suddenly see how in my earlier meditation on the visible aspects of aging—the marks of time on a woman's face at fifty—I had bracketed the rest. I seem to have missed a crisis about mortality: beyond the wound to vanity, the warning signs of approaching death itself—my own. I managed to miss this even though I was measuring my future life against the relatively early death of my mother (of course one is not strictly speaking young at sixty-eight, but the parents of many contemporaries are living well into their nineties). I was aware enough of the death watch actually to include in the essay a few passages from the book I had just finished, *Bequest and Betrayal: Memoirs of a Parent's Death*; I saw in those passages a reflection about what might carry over from one generation to the next, but even then something escaped me. I was once asked whether in addition to my own betrayal of my parents' lives by writing about them often harshly, I meant by "betrayal" that my parents had betrayed me by exiting from my life when, and especially how, they did. I confess that, preoccupied by what I took to be the daring of my truth-telling, I was not focused on their leaving. But now the answer seems stunningly obvious, although not perhaps what the questioner had in mind. Yes, no, I had not counted, not yet, on their loss. In retrospect I see how their loss bumped me up that much closer to my own mortality, reminded me that I, a middle-aged orphan (!), was next in line—and that maybe I wasn't all that ready either to lose them or to die. In a strange way that I don't fully understand even now, it took the publication of the book to bring that rupture home. Yes, I was alone and they were dead. The book proved it.

Returning to my thoughts about aging some five years later, I could say, updating Beauvoir's chronology, that by the time I recovered from the shock of turning fifty, I had reached sixty. And at sixty not only does fifty seem "young" but angsting over feathery lips or a crepey neck seems somewhat beside the point (though I'm not denying the point itself, of course). The real and now new point has to do (over and above the issue of face work) with my relation to death but also to my future work in the world (my job). To the extent that Beauvoir succeeded in coming to terms with her changing appearance and approaching death it was by saying—and continuing to act on the fact—that she was a writer. A writer keeps on writing. It's far easier to stretch your sagging flesh over your cheekbones with your fingers and imagine the effects of a face-lift (a minituck) than it is to contemplate the face of death—or worse still, the prospect of no more writing, no more useful work; and if not primarily a writer but, as is my case, a teacher whose writing has been tied to the academy, the specter of retirement.

Beauvoir went on to write a book about old age and to write more chapters of her memoirs in which she had time to meditate further on the meaning of age for her and others, on what had and hadn't changed in her life. Not many women writers have provided comparable meditations, if you are looking, as I am, for other ways of seeing. Marguerite Duras in her memoir, *The Lover*, describes the process of her premature aging while a still very young woman as something happening outside herself, as cultural material—a text.[20]

> My ageing was very sudden. I saw it spread over my features one by one, changing the relationship between them, making the eyes larger, the expression sadder, the mouth more final, leaving great creases in the forehead. But instead of being dismayed I watched this process with the same sort of interest I might have taken in the reading of a book. (4)

Steinem offers an American version of this French view at fifty in *Revolution from Within*, using other analogies but drawing the same conclusion (fig. 4.14).

> Looking in the mirror, I see the lines between nose and mouth that now remain, even without a smile, and I am reminded of a chipmunk storing nuts for the winter. When I

FIG. 4.14. Gloria Steinem by Andrea Renault.
Ms. Foundation Annual. Globe Photos, Inc. 200.

ask what they have to say for themselves, nothing comes back. They know I don't like them, so until I stop with the chipmunk imagery and learn to value them as the result of many smiles, they're not communicating. I'll have to work on this—and many other adjustments of aging still to come.   (248)

Like Solomon's autoportraits, the autobiographical narratives of Duras and Steinem offer the possibility of changing what you see in the mirror by changing your angle of vision, if not your life.

In my fifties I found that optimism ("something might be gained for women at the cusp of fifty," Heilbrun argues) both impossible to believe and cold comfort. This was a way of thinking available only to the exceptional beings who made these pronouncements, internationally recognized writers and public figures. I couldn't see how in the ordinariness of my life I would ever get over it. I could not be consoled by the shocked reactions of those to whom for one reason or another I confessed my age. Looking great for one's age has little to do with really looking good, I thought; besides, what was an interlocutor to say: fifty?! god, you look awful?

Sorting through some files of clippings I had saved about women and aging, I came upon a nasty review in *Vanity Fair* (under the rubric "Vanities") of another book of personal essays by Steinem, *Moving Beyond Words*.[21] The reviewer singled out "Doing Sixty" (misquoting): "By the time you read this, I'll be sixty. I realize now that fifty felt like leaving a much-loved and familiar country . . . but sixty feels like arriving at the border of a new one" (283). Steinem echoes Beauvoir's language but not her melancholy. "Yes, that's right," the reviewer (self-identified as a woman from another, younger generation) comments, "your teeth fall out and people beat you up more" (88).[22] Her greatest revulsion comes from Steinem's expressed faith in her inner child—and everyone else's—as a way of saving the world. To be sure, I could do without inner children myself, but what Steinem is trying out in this essay, trying on, are some new ways of talking about and living as a woman in one's age.

The title to Heilbrun's recent book *The Last Gift of Time: Life Beyond Sixty* is a provocation to acknowledge that there actually *is* life after sixty and that it might have something to offer.[23] Her most moving chapter, entitled "Time," concludes with a metaphor about time's gift. Commenting on a diary entry of Sylvia Townsend Warner's about spontaneously dancing for joy (at age sixty-nine) to a piece of music, Heilbrun writes: "The greatest oddity of one's sixties is that, if one dances for joy, one always supposes it is for the last time. Yet this supposition provides the rarest and most exquisite flavor to one's later years. The piercing sense of 'last time' adds intensity, while the possibility of 'again' is never quite effaced" (55).

What is the relation between last and again?

Beauvoir writes at the end of *Force of Circumstance*: "Yes, the time has come to say: Never again! It is not I who am saying good-bye to all those things I once enjoyed, it is they who are leaving me" (379). In 1963, the year in which *Force of Circumstance* was published, Beauvoir began an intense friendship with a younger woman. Sylvie le Bon (when Beauvoir adopted her, she added de Beauvoir to her name) was the person who encouraged her to write the book *A Very Easy Death* (1964), in which Beauvoir recounted her mother's illness and death that year. The relationship with Sylvie (thirty years younger than Beauvoir) transformed Beauvoir's life dramatically, including her sense of time and age: "There is such an interchange between us," Beauvoir writes in *All Said and Done*, "that I lose the sense of my age: she draws me forwards into her future, and there are times when the present recovers a dimension that it had lost" (72).

All Said and Done was published in 1972 when Beauvoir was sixty-four; it is dedicated to Sylvie. *The Last Gift of Time* is written from the perspective of a woman whose sixties are behind her but who has not closed the door to time's work. What lies on the other side of the door to one's sixties? Those of us who in the 1950s quivered to the suspense of quiz shows can remember the hope that a fabulous gift remained hidden behind the door and not the dreary consolation prize. The only way to find out is to choose a door, then wait for it to open, knowing that life itself is the reward.

(It's in only one's sixties, I think, that it becomes possible to see the anxiety about appearance that often haunts one's fifties as a way of displacing—or postponing—the crisis of mortality. Far easier to obsess about the signs of aging—the cosmetics of time's passage—than reflect upon death. Recently, my most intimate friend, my contemporary, and the one with whom for many years my life unfolded in an always complicated dialogue, died at age fifty-eight of a cerebral hemorrhage. We liked to tape our important conversations and called ourselves "les parleuses" in honor of Marguerite Duras's book by that name. Looking at her life from the decade of my sixties, it now seems to me that dying in one's fifties is dying young.

I open this parenthesis still in shock, in grief, and at the very beginning of the memory work that will help me try to make sense of this—her—story, that will help surround the loss with words. But on the edge of the gap I can already tell that the mirror is no longer where I will look to know what to make of what time remains.)

Moving through the mirror to contemplate the limits more than the marks of time, I feel another kind of urgency: this *is* my life, and so much of it is already in the past tense. Now what?

VANITAS VANITATUM

In her excoriating account of Steinem's "Doing Sixty," the reviewer rendered her sense of what's wrong with Steinem and her cohort, with them and their relations to younger feminists through a generational analogy: "Like beautiful and spirited daughters who fill their mothers with envy, the new wave of post-'70s feminists appears to have had a horrible effect on these childless grandmothers, who have suckled the enervating incubi of their inner children with an overcompensating vengeance which looks a lot like regret" (88). Over and above the characterization of an older generation of feminists as mothers envious of their daughters' beauty (uttered in a tone of identification with the beautiful daughters), the oxymoron of "childless grandmothers" ups the ante of resentment. It's as though childlessness continues to have its nonprocreative effects in the next generation. As opposed to the actual grandmothers fulfilled by their grandchildren and who represent an ideal (or at least better) model for women's aging, the embittered, childless grandmothers have only themselves to blame for their lack of satisfaction in how things have turned out.

(Perhaps the oxymoron is undone by the logic of stepfamilies. Looking at computers, I was asked by a salesman if I had children. When I said no, he said, what about grandchildren? If I had grandchildren, I would be interested in the feature that would allow me to receive photographs of the kiddies.)

The notion of the grandmother as a new ideal of attractive aging has recently surfaced in an item about Catherine Deneuve. In an interview titled "Showing Your Age Can Be a Beautiful Thing," the former English model Twiggy comments approvingly on the fact that "Catherine Deneuve—a 57-year-old grandmother—was last week appointed the new face of L'Oréal." But what's key here is not just the choice of Deneuve (the grandmother with her actual age) but the report that Deneuve has stipulated a " 'no airbrushing' clause in her contract."[24] There's a photo insert of a very glamorous Deneuve looking like a movie star and not your grandmother from central casting, so maybe it's time to update our ideas of what grandmothers look like (fig. 4.15). Still, I can't help feeling that not airbrushing the face of a beautiful woman, an exquisite face that has already been preserved from aging by strategic plastic surgery, is not quite the victory for older women and their role in advertising cosmetics that has so elated Twiggy (who also looks quite wonderful in the photo of her as the defender of female maturity).

In England, the senior citizen discount begins at sixty. I asked for one at a museum this past summer and the attendant—much to my chagrin—didn't look surprised. However much I complain about my aging face, stare into the mirror to survey the damage daily, when an objective observer shares my view, my vanity is wounded.

How can I be sixty when I'm twenty-eight inside?

FIG. 4.15. Catherine Deneuve by Allstar Picture Library.
Globe Photos, Inc. 200.

5

"Why Am I Not That Woman?"

A memory from "Saturday Night Live." When I was a beginning assistant professor in the seventies and living with someone who liked to stay up late, I used to watch this program, which was just getting started. In the news-update segment, Chevy Chase played the anchorman. At the start of his show he would look brightly into the camera and say, "Good evening. Welcome to the 7 o'clock news" and then, with palpable relish, sign on: "I'm Chevy Chase"— pause—"And you're not." It seemed pretty funny at the time.

I

> Listening to others means accepting that they
> are different from you, different from each other.
> —Philippe Lejeune, *Le Moi des demoiselles*

All autobiographical acts take place in the tensile space between what's the same and what's different, self and other—between Montaigne and Rousseau. I write, Reader, because I'm just like you; I write, Reader, because there's no one like me. A critic today negotiates more or less self-consciously between these two positions. But whatever your place in the map of that territory, writing about yourself puts your ego out there—*all alone*—in relation to the others who are your readers. On the border between the ego and the other is the potential for identification or repudiation, sympathy or revulsion, love or violence.

Annie Ernaux's life writing works that border. In three powerful and extremely successful family memoirs about her parents, *A Man's Place*, *A Woman's Story*, and *Shame*, Ernaux offers finely detailed portraits of provincial manners in postwar France that are also meditations on the nature of self-knowledge. Representing her parents' lives has also allowed Ernaux as a daughter to trace in counterpoint the transformation in her own life from the childhood memories of a café-épicerie, which her parents owned and ran, to the habits of a professional class to which as a writer and teacher she now belongs. In *Exteriors*, a collection of diary entries, she writes in the first person from the position of those who earn a living by teaching, talking about, or writing books, but she writes with a divided consciousness—with a loyalty to the voices and bodies of the past still present in her. The diary is a transcription of scenes witnessed and dialogues overheard in the unexpected encounters of public transportation, at the check-out counters at the supermarket—in the common spaces of the modern Parisian suburbs where Ernaux herself lives. The book is about what is one's own, what belongs to others; about how this always ragged division is a fact of language; and implicitly about how reading the facts of identity in language is what makes her a writer. Or, as she puts it in a throwaway parenthesis, "(I realize that I'm always looking for literature's signs in reality)" (41, TM).[1]

The book opens with an epigraph from Rousseau: "Our *true* self is not wholly in us."[2] The diary returns to that proposition in a variety of forms:

Why do I describe and detail this particular scene, like many others in the book? What is it I am desperately seeking in reality? ... Committing to paper the movements, postures and words of the people I meet gives me the illusion of being close to them. I don't speak to them, I only watch them and listen to them. Yet the emotions they arouse in me are real. I may also be trying to discover something about myself through them, their attitudes or their conversations. (Sitting opposite someone in a subway car, I often ask myself, *"why am I not that woman?"*).   (32; emphasis added)

What is it about the other person that makes me what I am? Writing about the people she sees allows the autobiographer to launch herself into the world and language.

Ernaux continues the mode of cultural criticism that Roland Barthes launched so brilliantly in *Mythologies* almost thirty years ago, although she is more preoccupied than he with the violence at work in the rhetoric of social distinctions. But despite the obvious difference in their class histories, they share in tone the loneliness of the observer Barthes poignantly stylized throughout his writing.

I bought a copy of *Marie-Claire* at the station in the New Town. This month's horoscope: "You will meet a wonderful man." Throughout that day I wondered if the man I was talking to was the one they meant.

(By choosing to write in the first person, I am laying myself open to criticism, which would not have been the case had I written "she wondered whether the man she was talking to was the one they meant." The third person—he/she—is always another, free to do whatever they choose. "I" is me, reader, and it's inconceivable—or unacceptable—for me to read my horoscope and behave like a shopgirl. "I" shames the reader ["Je" fait honte au lecteur]).   (17, TM)

The dare of " 'I' shames the reader" multiplies its effects in Ernaux's writing. The author chooses to run the risk (Rousseau-like) of revealing something embarrassing about herself, which in turn embarrasses the reader: makes the reader ashamed *for* the writer. It's more embarrassing still if the reader herself, say, consults her horoscope seriously enough to wonder if it might come true.

One way or another, class shame (tackiness, humiliation, or moral outrage) is almost always at the heart of Ernaux's social critique: "The President spoke on television last Sunday. On several occasions he used the expression 'little people' . . . as if the people he was referring to could neither see him nor hear him. . . . The president's speech also implied that he himself was to be bracketed with 'great people' " (35). This permanent undercutting of pretension gives her writing its specificity and, to evoke a phrase dear to Barthes, the voice its grain.

For Ernaux, what's most alive in others is what brings her back to herself.

> On other occasions, a woman waiting at a check-out counter would remind me of my mother because of the way she moved or spoke. It's therefore outside, in the subway passengers . . . or shoppers on the escalator at the Galeries Lafayette . . . that my past existence resides. In total strangers who have no idea that they possess part of my story; in faces and bodies I will never see again. In the same way, anonymous in the crowds in the streets and in the stores, I myself carry the lives of others (Je suis porteuse de la vie des autres).   (95, TM)

Suburban flâneuse at the end of the twentieth century, Ernaux is looked at as well as looking: shopper and shoppee.

In this mode of reciprocal relation articulated in the diary's final entry, the autobiographer's ego is incomplete without the anonymous individuals who, unbeknownst to them, fill her in, flesh her out. Writers or readers, Ernaux argues, we all need these faces in the crowd. Identity is a process of mutual composition that takes place over time spent among others and requires their participation. But once this reciprocity is recorded, the anonymous others become the writer's material. The others don't know the part they have in producing the writer's existence (although as her readers we, of course, do). The last sentence caps that discrepancy.

When I first read *Exteriors*, I wrote to Annie Ernaux asking her to clarify what she meant by the phrase "carrying the lives of others"—and (amazingly) she replied.[3]

> In fact I made a brutal discovery of reciprocity: the person I am, my face, gestures, voice, everything that I consider as uniquely "me," perhaps reminds anonymous others of a loved or hated person, or some earlier phase of their life. But the choice of the expression "carrying the life of others," was probably not innocent: it was also a way of identifying one of the book's meanings, as well as the role of the writer (that only comes to me now). Yes, the writer as bearer of signs, signs that are also, like sandwich boards, advertisements to be read by others, who themselves are bearer of signs.

In this sense, we the readers take up the place of the people who see the writer, who learn something about themselves from her. Once deciphered, "literature's signs in reality" become readable to all, repeatable and therefore able—as new signs—to bring the lives of others to others. In describing Ernaux's advertisements in my own story, I too produce signs for others to read; writing autobiography (and reading it) mitigates loneliness and removes the partitions that appear to wall off the self from empathy or compassion. "I'm no longer writing these words just for me," Ernaux remarks in *A Woman's Story*, faced with the anxiety caused by her mother's decline into the horrors of Alzheimer's disease. "I'm no longer writing just for me," she continues, "to make it bearable for myself, I'm writing so that others will understand" (80, TM).[4]

But despite the impulse to identify with the others you might in fact yet be ("why am I not that woman?"), your others are not necessarily your readers. They might not be readers at all. When "literature's signs in reality" are recorded on the page, the dream of symmetry is broken.

I ask the young woman who does my hair: "Do you like to read?" "Oh I don't mind reading," she replies, "but I don't have the time." ("I don't mind" washing the dishes, cooking, being on my feet all day—the expression is used to indicate that one is willing to do certain chores. It seems that reading is one of them.)   (68, TM)

The intellectuals among Ernaux's actual readers are probably the very people she least wishes to resemble. In *A Man's Place* Ernaux called the mode of writing she sought "flat writing" (l'écriture plate), the language without metaphors that she described as that of her parents' letters, a writing without the stylistic effects that bear the marks (affectations) of another class.[5]

On the phone, M.—a redhead with glasses, a fur coat in winter—in her intellectual and peremptory voice: "You need a cat. You can't be a writer without a cat." Last week, J-C. L., a literary critic: "You can tell a real writer from his notebooks." So writing isn't enough; there have to be external signs, material evidence to define what a "real" writer is. Yet in fact these signs are available to everyone.   (46, TM)

This diary of life lived outside, in public, in democratic spaces, works at refusing the gap between the writer and her others. Ernaux takes as her material the transitory exchanges of everyday life, what's available to everyone, what belongs to the excluded "little people." And yet every entry bears the poignant traces of the inevitable divide: what's not shared or what reveals class distinctions. With every transcription the writer can't help crossing over. By becoming a writer Ernaux moved irrevocably away from what she called at the end of *A Woman's Story* "the world ruled by words and ideas" to the world of those who exercise a certain power through words and ideas, the world where her mother had "wanted [her] to live" (91). Writing, therefore, does separate you from yourself; once you put yourself on paper, there's no going back. Does that mean that you should adjust to that world? Take yourself for one of the "great people"?

When I was in graduate school, I had the impression that our teachers (the ones we most admired) were somehow saying: "I'm Chevy Chase, and you're not." It wasn't all that funny in real life (not that you could always tell the difference), but since we girls were committed masochists, it seemed a fair enough gloss of our relations. (No self-respecting feminist teacher would today admit to longing for those violent subject/object positions, reminding students of their place. On the other hand, I recognize the temptation.)

You can't become a teacher, any more than you can become a writer, without running the risk of occupying the place and borrowing the language of those who most bothered you in your earliest gestures of identification (or admiration). The problem is not simple because it has to do with the insecurity of the categories themselves: if we think we know who others are to us, we can't, as it turns out, always know who we are to others. We can't know truly who we are to ourselves because, as Rousseau goes on to add, "others have their part in us." This intractable incompleteness of knowledge (which others, when, how?) means that selfhood (like identity) remains a process that is neither entirely free nor wholly overdetermined. It's therefore in the constant adjustment between ego and other, and in the recognition that the process is always reversible, that any ethical form of relation must take root.

II

Listening to others, obviously, leads to identification.
—Philippe Lejeune, *Le Moi des demoiselles*

Seven years after *Exteriors*, Annie Ernaux published a second installment of her public diary-keeping, *La Vie extérieure*.[6] Dated

1993–1999, these entries, like those from earlier years (1985–1992), derive their material from an engagement with the world as a recognizable social, even literary, text that can be deciphered and read. The diary is collaborative, as she sees it, collective in its making; almost as if, Ernaux writes on the book's back jacket, she had no part in its composition. And yet, she concludes, "I also know that more than in a personal diary, my own story and figures that look like me emerge from these notations of my external life." This documentation functions both as a historical framework for her individual story and a kind of vast community theater that provides the actors in it (locals, citizens) with a chance alternately to star on stage and to sit in the audience. Above all, the diarist observes the world with the habits of a postmodern participant/observer in the field of her life, studying the artifacts of her own culture without a will to narrative—jotting down "moments in time, chance meetings"—a kind of "ethnowriting" (*Exteriors* 56).

Continuing the work of *Exteriors*, Ernaux in *La Vie* lays bare the emotional logic that connects her to others: the process by which perceiving one's relation to the other reveals something, even teaches one something, about oneself. Overhearing a conversation on the train to Paris, for instance, in which a man asks a young woman details about her job, the writer indirectly justifies the role of the diary: "to learn about other people's lives so that we can learn about our own life or the life we might have chosen" (49). The diaries offer a pedagogy of self-discovery through the other, not so much psychological as anthropological, what she called in her memoir *Shame* an "ethnological study of the self"[7] (33). Ernaux's ethics of autobiographical engagement echo Virginia Woolf's well-known description in *Moments of Being* of the problems involved in describing a life: "Consider what immense forces society brings to play on each of us, how that society changes from decade to decade; and also from class to class; well, if we cannot analyse these invisible presences, we know very little of the subject of the memoir; and again how futile life-writing becomes" (80).[8] Ernaux is fascinated by the visible traces of those forces.

A woman catches her eye on a flight from Marseilles to Paris:

her clothing, her gestures (not reading but filing her nails instead, checking her face in her mirror), her decision to buy a glass of champagne and savor it.

> A woman is going to meet a man. She treats herself to the champagne to complete the pleasure of anticipation. To celebrate the anticipation itself.
> Before the plane lands, she looks at herself again in the mirror, fixes her makeup. It's as though I were she.   (13)

As Ernaux studies the woman looking at herself in the mirror, she joins her desire. It's not the face itself but the gesture of looking that causes the identification. I could be in her place. The woman-mirror also looks back and supplies information in reverse: she tells me something about myself, my way of taking pleasure. But could she be me?

In another moment of witness, Ernaux watches a woman handling a package of pantyhose in a department store. Suddenly, she realizes that the woman was in fact in the process not of shopping but of stealing—stuffing a pair of pantyhose into her bag. Fleetingly, Ernaux identifies with the shoplifter: "I imagined the heady sensation of this woman" (14). Again, she puts herself in the other woman's place and experiences feelings not her own. It's almost as though she tries on another's identity, sometimes leaping over the boundaries that separate, collapsing the difference. The text is punctuated by these bursts of identification through which feeling another's desire calls up a response from one's own body present and past. The vicarious becomes visceral.

A crowd is descending into the metro station at Auber. From the steps of the escalator a couple is glimpsed embracing. Then a train pulls in, and the man and the woman part, running to catch the train. "They were exactly at the spot where, one evening last year, toward midnight, I was with F. Like the woman, I had my back against the wall. The escalator kept moving, endlessly, empty of travelers, with a perpetual clicking" (24). The woman leaning against the wall rewards Ernaux with a flashback from her own life.

No narrative, no trip down memory lane, no story. The diary entry flickers and offers a novelistic scene—a novelist's scene—and leaves the reader there, perhaps with a flash of her own: the only time when having your back up against the wall is a state of pleasure. The unknown woman supplies a kind of living mnemonic.

In these examples, as in many others over these years of the diary, the trigger is the act of a woman who in some way reminds Ernaux of herself, a woman in a mood of desire, attracted by the heightening of sensation, of crossing lines, especially those of bourgeois propriety. But the movement from the scene observed to the singular memory does not necessarily require the figure of an obvious double: a woman just like me, even if that's the instance I began with in order to make the clearest case. Later in the day of the plane trip, when Ernaux watches a group of black musicians performing on the street in Paris, she is inhabited by a youthful longing: "I remember the dream I had when I was sixteen, of going to live in Harlem, because of jazz" (13). To the extent that someone in the picture stands in for the writer in the Parisian street scene, it's a drunken white man, lost in himself, dancing to the music.

Often Ernaux's strongest identifications are cross-identifications: almost literally putting herself in the other's place. In this sense, reading Ernaux is to be reminded of these unexpected proximities—of the possibility of being like those whom one does not resemble. In other words, the diaries enact on the reader's behalf an ethics of disidentification, which is perhaps autobiography's greatest gift.

Unlike the memoir, which requires the shaping of narrative and the retrospective interpretation of the past, the diary reports out of order, responding randomly to the demands and accidents of the present tense. Flashes of intensity may in time fade into future absences. Thus, in rereading her diary entries, Ernaux discovers she has already forgotten many of the events recorded in its pages, even her own acts of authorship; perhaps she's "not the one who transcribed them." Nonetheless, whatever the prosthetic failure of the diary (it can't remember *for* you), the diary never stops performing that work of observation—the will to record the outside world, to seize its reality.

But if as readers we are tempted to identify with Ernaux, it can only be with the writer not the person. And not with the biographical writer either, who may not even be "the one who transcribed" the events we read. *La Vie* is curiously, if deliberately, lacking in the kind of biographical detail readers might expect or secretly crave. Having been locked out, we want in despite the fact that we've been warned that the door to the domains of intimate life will stay closed. On November 30, 1997, Ernaux recounts a weekend her son and his girlfriend spent at her house watching the *X-Files*, playing computer games, going to the mall. And yet, if she does her son's laundry, irons his T-shirts, the personal anecdote quickly turns generic, almost sociological: "I note here the signs of an era, nothing individual: the Sunday of a woman alone whose son comes to visit her with his girlfriend, near Paris" (88–89). The writer is a woman, a woman alone, but what matters is less the personal content of that category than the category itself: "woman alone, Sunday": or even "Sunday, see under woman alone."

More typically, the portrait of the writer comes by indirection, as in the account of Iranian writer Taslima Nasreen's appearance at the Pompidou Center. This is a full-court press conference, and Nasreen takes questions about her role as a writer. Does she, for example, believe that there's such a thing as women's writing. "She answers that women are more observant than men, that they need to find their own language and that she's not feminist but humanist" (49). Ernaux doesn't comment on the answer (or the question), though one can imagine Ernaux answering a question about women's writing in a similar fashion—at least on the basis of the diaries.

Ernaux tells the story of giving money to an alcoholic begging on the steps of the subway station near her home. He's clearly wasted by poverty and alcoholism, and he smells awful. He wishes her a Merry Christmas when she gives him money, and she returns the greeting as if they were having a conventional exchange of holiday pleasantries. Immediately afterward, Ernaux berates herself for joining the charade of bourgeois politeness that ignores the gross disparity between a man huddled among garbage bags and a woman shopping for a holiday dinner. "I feel so disgusted with myself that to erase the shame I wish I could wrap myself in his coat, kiss his hands, smell his breath" (61). Here, rather than the almost automatic and pleasurable jolt of identification with the woman on the plane fixing her makeup in the mirror, or the woman in the department store stealing the pantyhose, the violence of disidentification is so powerful that Ernaux in fantasy desperately longs to break the sense of social distance that separates her from the *clochard* by creating physical intimacy.

It's through the marks of outer difference that Ernaux often learns the most about herself—often what she might not want to know, or what she likes least about herself. What, she wonders, on another occasion, would she prefer to do for money if she found herself impoverished: begging or "prostitution, public shame or private shame. The need to measure myself against extreme forms of dereliction, as if there were a truth one could only learn at that price" (111). "People and their lives pass through me" (Je suis traversée par les gens) Ernaux writes with a peculiar but not uncharacteristic provocation in *Exteriors*, "like a whore" (62, TM). The deadening lock of social role is the behavior Ernaux most despises in modern culture—a studied and incorporated indifference that never ceases to grab her attention and that she insists upon, almost hungrily cataloguing her own guilty participation.

By far the largest category of references in *La Vie* is that of public spaces where Ernaux perceives herself as just an actor among others. In the supermarket the (women) cashiers greet you when they touch the first item you are buying. "In the eyes of the marketing people, we exist only in that momentary transaction between detergent . . . and our money" (47). This banality about consumerism in daily life generates a rare comment about the writer's task: "The always vain hope of having nothing more to note, to not be caught up by anything in the outside world, in this mass of anonymous beings I encounter and to whom, for others, I belong" (47). Faced with the imperative both to record experience as an enmeshment with the world and to experience the ineluctability of that entanglement, Ernaux suddenly registers a kind of lassitude.

But if the requirement to be present to others (to look and be seen) can weary, it also provides a protection against the dissolution of the self.

Today, for a few minutes, I tried to *see* all the people I encountered, all strangers. It seemed to me that their existence, by the detailed observation I made of their being, suddenly became very close to me, as if I touched them. If I were to continue this experiment, my vision of the world and of myself would be radically changed by it. Perhaps I would no longer have a self.　　(26)

The unremitting gaze comes at a cost to one's own ego boundaries.

Ernaux is moved by a twin desire for self-effacement—escaping into the life, whether of a specific other (a shoplifter, a drunk) or anonymous others, of merging—and at the same time for separateness, remaining distinct, defined, and delineated as an individual. Perhaps to be a writer—a life writer—entails just this alternation between immersion and separation. Without the others one doesn't exist; but with too much awareness of others one's ego vanishes into the crowd. The bind is double because it is not solely a question of the observer's take on the world. The writer is trapped in an involuntary reciprocity; the writer's body, as we saw earlier, also signifies to and for others.

Writer's body, woman's body. To what extent are the choices of material Ernaux makes hers dependent on a memory housed in a woman's body? I return to the question the journalists put to Naslima Nasreen about the existence of women's writing. If women, as Nasreen answered, are more observant than men, what kinds of thing do they observe? The last entry of Ernaux's diary, November 4, 1999, describes a mural from the 1970s at the local train station that portrays a man and a woman embracing. "On the dress, at the place where her genitals would be, someone has thrown red paint which looks like a splash of blood" (131). The diary ends there with no comment. Just the image of a bloodied woman's body.

Ernaux locates herself in passing through a spectrum of identifications and disidentifications between other women and herself: "Why am I not that woman?" "It's as though I were she." "I imagined the heady sensation of this woman." "Like the woman, I had my back against the wall." If there's an implicit bridge linking the women cashiers and shoppers (Ernaux among them), between Ernaux and women who live out their sexual desire; if there's a certain commonality, even a bodily one, this does not add up to a solidarity of experience that crosses all boundaries. Rather, identification in the diaries (with women or not) is an intermittent act, a social performance driven by desire or disgust and punctuated by specific moments of history—local (a splash of red paint) or international. Ernaux's view of the difference that being a woman makes in the examination of any individual's responsibility as a European citizen (her primary emphasis in *La Vie*) remains ambiguous. The death of Princess Diana is a case in point. Who cares, and should we?

September 1, 1997

Diana died with her lover in a car crash at the Alma Bridge, Saturday night. Contrast with the enormous collective emotion generated by Diana's death and the indifference toward the dozens massacred in Algeria. . . . She had a story we [*on*] followed for years, and with which a huge number of women identified: a princess but like us [*nous*]. The story of the anonymous Algerians begins with their death.   (84–85)

The princess is like us—women; the Algerians are not. Why is it so difficult to cross the borders of the self to identify with those not like us? Part of the problem resides in the disparity between those with an autobiography (the story of the proper name) and those with a collective, unauthored story.

Identification or indifference, there is (should be) no way for a solitary ego to reside in isolation within the social world, if we accept (as Ernaux does) Rousseau's view of identity outside of nature. For Rousseau natural man is wholly autonomous: "Natural man is entirely for himself. He is numerical unity, the absolute whole which is in relation only to itself or its kind";[9] but when Rousseau defines the self constituted through civic bonds, it is as a relational being: "Our sweetest existence is relative and collective, and our true *self* is not entirely within us" (118).[10] Are there models of relation that escape those of hierarchy or aggression between ego and others? Yes. But they require a constant reminder of reciprocal dependency, the porousness and vulnerability of personal boundaries. Nothing easier than forgetting what is shared. Once the bond of potential identification frays, the ego's childhood wish to stand alone, invulnerable, floods back, dampening the urge to recognize the others in its view, caught in the fantasy of self-sufficiency.

So when you get down to it, however vigilant about its readers, autobiography remains the act of that solitary ego asserting the right (or need) to take up room in the public spaces of reading and writing. Whatever reciprocity may be wished for from readers, readers remain the audience, unless they in turn produce autobiographical writing of their own. Until then the author's signature remains a particular kind of sign on the page and in the world, a sign difficult to ignore: Reader, pay attention to me. At the same time, as I've been insisting, since autobiography works through a system of checks and balances, the reader, of course, always has the option to withhold recognition, to leave the author dead on the page, cocooned in egotism. And that's an autobiographical act all its own.

Epilogue: My Grandfather's Cigarette Case, or What I Learned in Memphis

> Jack asked me, Isn't it a terrible thing to grow up in the shadow of another person's sorrow?
>
> I suppose so, I answered. As you know, I grew up in the summer sunlight of upward mobility. This leached out a lot of that dark ancestral grief.
>
> —Grace Paley, "The Immigrant Story"

At the end of my last book I left myself standing in the cemetery where my parents and paternal grandparents are buried. Contemplating the two sets of graves after my father's death, I fantasized selling the burial plot that my father had bought for me. I didn't want to end up there, I thought, sandwiched between the untended graves (between my parents again—or was it still?), captioned by epitaphs—beloved this, devoted that—coded language that revealed little of a story that had gone very wrong a long time ago. Mainly I wanted to stop wondering about the metaphorical family plot whose twists and turns had kept me preoccupied, not to say knotted up, for so much of my life. The Kipnis mystery would remain locked away behind the ornate iron gates of the Manhattan Fraternal Association (a workingman's organization that obtained burial plots for poor immigrants) from which my grandparents had bought their place in the cemetery. And I would, as they say, move on.

What *was* their story? Why did they seem so unknown, unknowable? Writing myself out of a literal dead end, I hoped, would also mean an end to a certain style of predictable misery, reliving the scenarios of family romances. But even if I *could* sell my own plot (which as it turned out, I couldn't), my very own place in the crowded company of Jews who had wound up in Flushing, Long Island, what would that accomplish? And what made me think I could offer back the story along with it?

"From the time that Abraham bought the cave at Machpelah to bury Sarah," Ruth Gay observes in *Unfinished People*, "there has been one kind of real estate that every Jew has bought, and that is a cemetery plot."[1] There is also a kind of real estate many immigrant Jews like my grandparents bought in the early decades of the twentieth century.

Land, tiny plots of land in Palestine.

In the summer of 2000 I was contacted by a man with information about an inheritance. My paternal grandparents, he said, had owned property that my sister and I were entitled to. The old joke about selling the Brooklyn Bridge almost passed my lips; it would not have been the first time I was conned. But the man was not asking us to write checks. My father's parents were poor, I said skeptically; when they first came to New York they lived in a tenement on the Lower East Side (where else?). What could they have left for anyone to inherit? Property in Russia, I said, in the shtetl? An initialed silver cigarette case that had belonged to my grandfather, a fork and spoon engraved with Russian letters: that was my inheritance, an immigrant's legacy. What if your grandparents had given money to a Zionist organization? A small sum as a mitzvah? What if that good deed had turned into property of value? Considerable value!

I remembered the contents of a manilla legal folder marked in capital letters "Property in Israel and Shendel Kipnis"—with "and Sadie Kip" scrawled in pencil, added sometime later. I kept the folders along with other such ephemera that autobiographers guard with their lives—superannuated stock certificates, old checkbooks, snapshots of people I had never met.

He saved; I saved.

The phone call vindicated both of us. The folder contained: a Certificate of Registration issued by the Palestine Government, Land Registry Office of Jerusalem; a contract in the name of Shendel Kipnis residing at 141 Stanton Street, NYC, recording payment in the amount of $350 for two dunams of land from the Nachlas Itschak Co. of Houston Street; a blue map with numbered plots indicating the location of the parcels in the Village of Souba, Palestine; four canceled checks dated March, June, November, and December 1926, signed by my grandfather, R. H. Kipnis; a brief correspondence from May 1949 between my father and a friend of his in real estate who had gone to Israel and discussed the possible reacquisition of this property from its previous owner ("at one time part of [his] ancestral property"); an exchange with said owner signaled by an empty envelope covered with Israeli stamps (and postage due); and, finally, a recommendation by the friend that my father "hang on to the land for some time" if he didn't need the money because the dunams were located "directly in the middle of the new plan for Jerusalem." My father had never mentioned this property to me; maybe the scribbled "Sadie Kip" meant that he intended to; maybe he had sold it. I returned the folder to my filing cabinet and chalked up the vanished investment to my father's legendary inability to seize the financial occasion.

But this is not the point of my story, even if I would love to (and may yet) have a small, belated inheritance. The half-acre plot of land is only the literal manifestation of the plot whose through line has revived the enigma of my father's family. I describe, in chapter 2, with a deliberate insouciance, giving up the Kipnis name and taking the name Miller, my mother's. The Kipnis line, I thought, seemed so dead-ended, distant, whereas the descendants of the Miller family were still alive. Not that I reasoned that way in 1974; family ties were the least of my concerns. Then, taking the Miller name felt like a kind of self-reinvention—leaving behind an old skin mottled by a past I rejected. This feminist gesture was not, it now strikes me, so unlike that of the many Jewish immigrants who, like the Millers themselves, gladly relinquished the name that marked them as foreign and tied them to a history they actively wished forgotten. I was following the immigrants from whom I descended. Moreover, I didn't know of any Kipnises, beyond, of course, the world-famous one, Alexander the basso (and later his son, Igor, a harpsichordist)—to whom, my father sometimes hinted when we were growing up, we were very distantly related. (Alexander Kipnis came from the same corner of the world my grandparents did, and from the photographs on the record jackets of the many albums my father collected, you could sort of see, if you were looking for it, a family resemblance: big, square heads.)

Suddenly, the Kipnis name was back in my life story. The conditions for the inheritance stipulated that all the heirs be found. My grandparents had two sons, my father and my father's older brother, who had moved to Arizona because of his son's asthma. If it seems strange to me now that I had never met my uncle and first cousin and more peculiar still that my father no longer saw his brother, it didn't then. We accepted the internal Kipnis family blanks without pressing for explanations, along with the other mysteries—such as *where* they really came from, when, what they did for a living (the "why" they left was the portmanteau pogrom and generic Cossacks that carried a weight of causality always tossed about lightly, with a kind of shrug or wave—what could you expect?). Until her death when my sister and I were young, Grandma Kipnis appeared a remote figure who baked sugar cookies (irregular, broken-off pieces of flat dough—shapeless but still delicious) that she offered in lieu of conversation on our rare visits to the Bronx, where the family seemed to have moved sometime in the 1930s. My grandfather had died before my parents married.

Among my father's papers I found a résumé from the 1960s belonging to my cousin, whom I tried to contact after my father's death. I dialed the phone number listed with an address in Tennessee from 1960; his ex-wife gave me a post office box number in Texas. I wrote, but the letter never reached its destination.

The conditions for the inheritance required that I find him. Was he still alive? I knew from my grandmother's obituary (a tiny clipping glued onto a torn index card) that my cousin had a daughter.

I returned to the résumé. This time I connected—both with the cousin, who had remarried and moved back to Memphis, and with his daughter. When I reached my cousin on the phone, he said, you're the one who went to Paris. To his ex-wife I was Uncle Lou's daughter. One phone call, and I was right back in the Kipnis story; in fact I used that name in order to introduce myself.

I flew to Memphis. I learned from my cousin's daughter, who was interested in family genealogy, that a Kipnis Web site existed (!). From it, she had obtained the names of the ships my grandparents (Raphael and Shendel), uncle (Shulem), and great-grandfather (earlier with his wife) had traveled on to America from Kishinev, as well as the addresses of their destinations in New York. I had never known about this great-grandfather—Chaim Hirsch Kipnis—who, according to the ship's manifest for the *Southwark*, was a carpenter by profession and could also read and write. I remembered having seen a photograph, which my cousin had in her album, not a snapshot but a posed, professional family portrait including him: a skinny man with a long pointy beard and a tall black hat, seated around a table with my grandfather and uncle; my cousin as a child sat perched upon the table. Kipnis generations minus my father (so where was my father?). This great-grandfather looked like a caricature of the Jewish immigrant from Eastern Europe at the turn of the century. On Raphael's death certificate, Chaim had become Harry. According to the Web site, Chaim's wife, Sure (Sarah on the death certificate), of Bratslav (like her husband), appears to have traveled the next month on the *Rotterdam*; destination in New York, 28 Delancey Street, where her husband, Chaim, resided. Of this great-grandmother I have found no further trace—neither narrative nor visual.

(No sooner do I write this, than I realize that it's not true that I had never known; I just had not picked up the thread. I suddenly remember the letter my sister and I found among my father's papers, a letter that my uncle had written to our father on the occasion of their mother's death and that my sister read at our father's funeral in the place of a eulogy. In the letter, my uncle recalled the words their father ["Pop"] had uttered after *his* father's funeral. So

I *could* have known about that "Grandpa," though still too late to have found anything out. Why, why this silence? What couldn't my father tell?)

With all this new knowledge, what exactly did I know? Did this bring me any closer to the so-called truth that autobiographers (including me) dream of? What could I *do* with this information? Was this the longed for key to the mystery of the family plot? I could go to Israel to inspect my dunams. I could go down to 96 Allen Street and see (possibly) the tenement that my grandfather had given the immigration officers as his father's address. And if I did that, what more would I know? But here's the worst thing: the only person who would have been interested in my discoveries, who would have appreciated the irony but also the fact of this belated enthusiasm for my Jewish Kipnis roots, was my father, the person who had left me clues that I had filed away rather than pursue.

(So I write that—throwing up my hands—and then I think, why not go downtown to see? If, by the time I went to look for it, 141 Stanton Street no longer existed, the same might not be true for 96 Allen Street. What had I to lose?)

I found and didn't find 96 Allen Street. The address is no longer attached to a building but to the theater exit of the Lower East Side Tenement Museum. The actual building is gone—destroyed when Allen Street was broadened to accommodate traffic in 1932—but in the early part of the century, it stood back-to-back with 97 Orchard Street, now the location of the museum. The discovery brings its own frustrations. I love this physical proximity to my origins: being close in these matters is not as good as the real thing, but it seems to be as close as I ever get. The tenement my grandparents went to upon their arrival in New York—perhaps where my father was born—represents exemplary immigrant life at the turn of the century. I can tour the museum and imagine my grandparents' home; I can study the floor plan, if not of their apartment then that of their neighbors with whom they would have shared a backyard. The pleasure brought by this fact, as well as the *idea* of the museum, overrides the less attractive information about Allen

Street that I read in the guidebooks to the Lower East Side—a dark street in the shadow of the El, "a disreputable thoroughfare of vice and poverty," and notorious for its red-light district.[2] Still it's also true that I can't quite shake off a certain melancholy—that sense of perpetual belatedness, which is perhaps the definition of autobiography.

Until now I had failed to go on the treasure hunt of lost origins that might have illuminated the generational chain. Years ago my father had walked over to his local library and photocopied subject indexes from the *New York Times* of 1903 and 1905 and starred in red the references to the famous (though not then to me, in what had to be willful ignorance) Kishinev massacres. He had also copied part of a map from an atlas showing where Kishinev was located.

Had I only followed the paper trail, I would have learned what happened in the Easter massacre of 1903, a massacre reported in the *New York Times* as "worse than the censor will permit to publish":

> The mob was led by priests, and the general cry, "Kill the Jews," was taken up all over the city. The Jews were taken wholly unaware and were slaughtered like sheep. The dead number 120 and the injured about 500. The scenes of horror attending this massacre are beyond description. Babes were literally torn to pieces by the frenzied and bloodthirsty mob. The local police made no attempt to check the reign of terror. At sunset the streets were piled with their corpses and wounded. Those who could make their escape fled in terror, and the city is now practically deserted of Jews.
>
> (April 28, 1903)

My favorite article from that year indulges in unexpected irony: "Kishineff as a City: Far from a Bad Place to Live in, Except for a Jew" (June 7, 1903).

Other pogroms were reported in 1905. One headline reads: "Odessa Jews Panic-Stricken. Believe a Massacre is Planned—Alarm at Kishineff Also." Easter holidays were a particularly anxious time. Under the article dated April 25, 1905, describing circulars in the streets of Odessa calling on people to kill the Jews, is the report of a countermessage: "Archbishop Vladimir preached a sermon yesterday admonishing the Christians to refrain from violence and manifestations of race hatred during the festivals of peace." But Easter wasn't the only trigger. A wave of pogroms related to the upheaval of the First Russian Revolution took place in the fall of 1905.[3]

In April 1906, the following year, my grandparents and eight-year-old uncle arrived in New York with $100. My father was born that December. (And now I think I know where.)

As always, I am left with unanswerable questions. Did Raphael and Shendel or Schulem witness the massacres? Did they tell my father this story?

Maybe they remained speechless.

(According to my cousin's daughter, her grandfather, my uncle, laughed about being given rides by the Cossacks when they passed through the town on horseback.)

In 1903 the rubric "Race or People" was added to the categories of a ship's manifest, after that of nationality. The first twenty-one names on the *Potsdam* were listed as "Hebrew."

There's a photograph I acquired on my trip to Memphis of my grandfather, father, and cousin standing in front of an iron mesh gate to a small, fenced-in park. My grandfather is wearing a straw bowler and a bow tie, a pleated shirtfront with a stand-up collar, a vest, and a long jacket. My father is sporting a fedora, a suit with a regular tie, and a pocket handkerchief. Both are smoking (finally, the origin of my obsessive smoking, an atavism: Kishinev was famous for its tobacco fields, and one version of my new information had my grandfather as a tobacconist). My cousin, a small child, is dressed in a sailor outfit—middy blouse and sailor's cap—and is pulling apart one of those big, doughy, salted New York pretzels that sits in your gut like the lump of dough that it is.

Guessing at the dates, this would appear to be the mid-twenties. My father would be about eighteen: I had never before seen a photograph of him at this age (my father before he met my mother), a slender boy. This must be close to the time that

Shendel/Sadie bought the dunams in Palestine. They all look spiffy. Maybe, even if they were living on Stanton street, in the shadow of the Williamsburg bridge, they were doing well—already upwardly mobile in accordance with the immigrant plot.

In this photograph, where my grandfather and father are smoking, my grandfather is holding a shiny object between his thumb and index finger. I want to believe, and why not, that this is the silver cigarette case, engraved with his initials RHK (my sister's initials), which is now in my possession and that had reached me (my cousin told me) through a chain (of chain-smokers): from father to son, son to son, son to uncle (my father), father to me (actually, I appropriated it).

As I plunge into the archives, I am less rather than more satisfied. For beyond the cigarette case, I have only the story, no matter the version. I know a lot more than I did standing in the cemetery. And yet I want so, so much more. Wouldn't you?

When I reread these chapters, I see over and over again the struggle to reinhabit the body of the girl who was conned, the graduate student discovering the meaning of the binary opposition or her professor's hand down her blouse. If wishing won't make it true, writing it won't either. I want to coincide with my story, live inside it. And yet the more facts I discover, the more belated I feel. And not only because the files have vanished or the sources died. However close you get—more documents, more photographs, more stories—there's always a gap separating you from what you want to know. Whose long, tight, copper-colored curls (my father's?) are preserved in a broken cardboard box bearing the label "Savon violette"? Is that the same (*my*) cigarette case between Raphael's fingers?

Is it or is it not the cigarette case? That's only where my troubles begin. The new stories (what I learned in Memphis) baffle me. Was my uncle, having left school early and being good with numbers, really a bookie for the Cotton Club in Harlem, working for a Jewish gangster, Dutch Schultz, his son's godfather? I have trouble making this movie fit with my story of the (quiet, refined) Kipnises (my grandfather a bookkeeper, according to the records). And yet.

At first I was shocked (no wonder the brothers didn't visit each other), then, realizing that I probably would never be able to verify this information (the Mafia connection), elated by the comic turn. In other words, maybe this wasn't necessarily the bad news.

There is a pleasure, I've come to feel, in not being sure—not only in not knowing what you almost know but also in not knowing what you don't know you don't know. Just one year ago I had no idea that these dunams actually existed on more than a seventy-five-year-old map; that the map represented real real estate. It's not just about not knowing what might happen (the shared banality of fate, the suspense of merely living; I probably don't really want to know what I'm going to die of, or when). I enjoy the experience of being brought up against what I don't know that has *already* happened. (For instance, this might seem perverse, or a form of victim envy, but having been finally moved to sort out the immigration narrative that shaped me, thinking about Kishinev, makes me feel less adrift. I can see how I exist in historical time. That sounds kind of pretentious even to me, and yet there's an emotional force in the sense of lineage, however ghostly, this rerouting produces. Time and space are collapsed when I read about the Kishinev pogroms in the pages of my local paper, the *New York Times.*)

More and more I take comfort in not knowing my own story because of the joys of the uncertainty principle but also because I find that it's not mine alone. Others have their part in it. The presence of others—whether through intimacy or the proximity of generations—expands the material, lends ballast to a diminishing self. This has a double advantage: it provides new stories and unexpected connections. When my cousin's daughter told me about the Web site (an oxymoron, I would have thought, with such a name, and yet I was visitor 5917 to www.Kipnis.org as of the last update in 1999), I logged on to a map of multiple destinies that relocated my own. When I corresponded with the girl who had shared my con-man adventure, and she helped me with her diaries and photographs (a writer, she saved too), she was also telling me *her* story (in fact, she considered the experience *her* story as well as mine).

The benefit of this view of life writing, not to say life, is that it assuages the anxiety that always threatens the enterprise of going public with private stories: that it's only about you and so what. There is no way to tell a story that's only about you. I remind myself of this at every line. It's not just about me. Or else I've failed. Which of course I can't know until I've told it.

We read the lives of others to figure out how to make sense of our own, and in the process we also admit to our wishes for a future. So what may look like a stubborn attachment to the past is just as powerfully a passion for what is to come in all its unknowablity. Life writing is a way of moving forward into the future by revisiting the past—visiting and not getting stuck there, not taking up residence. If reading the stories of other people teaches anything, it's a lesson about time and timeliness—or is it untimeliness? A lesson about knowing that the life on the page has already changed—even before you have time to finish reading.

At the end of *Roland Barthes by Roland Barthes* (a self-portrait, written near sixty), the author looks for a way to end without ending: "And afterward?—What to write now? Can you still write anything?—One writes with one's desire, and I am not through desiring."[4] Resisting the inevitability of closure, the convention, however fictional, of the biographical narrative that requires a summing up, Barthes signals instead the prospect of more writing. Writing against death. Like memory, which is itself a reconstruction, memory's biography records a desire for what can never be fully known—your parents before you were born, who you are to others, all that is and isn't you—a desire, finally, for more words.

The cigarette case carries both a trace of the past and a warning about the future. Always a memento mori, the keepsake belonging to another is a reminder to the one who saves it. ("You must not forget anything," is the line that ends Philip Roth's *Patrimony*, the memoir of his father's death, written as the author approached sixty).[5] In other words, a memento invites you to reflect upon how to live now—with others.

This is why, I guess, I remain attached to these small proofs of a past that cannot remain buried anymore than the future can be predicted: a map of where I've come thus far and in whose company.

NOTES

I. BUT ENOUGH ABOUT ME, WHAT DO YOU THINK OF MY MEMOIR?

1. "Autocritography" is a term coined by Henry Louis Gates Jr. and developed by Michael Awkward in *Scenes of Instruction* (Durham: Duke University Press, 1999): "Autocritography . . . is an account of individual, social, and institutional concerns that help to produce a scholar and, hence, his or her professional concerns" (7). Daphne Patai, "Point of View," *Chronicle of Higher Education* (February 23, 1994): "I doubt that I am the only one who is weary of the nouveau solipsism—all this individual and collective breast-beating, grandstanding, and plain old egocentricity" (A52).

2. Jeffrey Williams, "The New Belletrism," *Style* 33, no. 3 (fall 1999): 414–42, 417.

3. I'd like to thank Caroline McCracken for inviting me to The Conference on English, "Remembered Lives," University of Wyoming, June 1999, for which I wrote this defense of the memoir.

4. *The Woman Warrior: Memoirs of A Girlhood Among Ghosts* (1976; reprint, New York: Vintage International, 1989), 5–6.

5. This act of finding oneself through the memories of others is an effect of what Susan Suleiman has called "autobiographical reading": "What exactly

am I looking for, and finding, in these works? I did not lose a parent during the war—yet I recognize the stories all too well. They could have been my own" (207). *Risking Who One Is: Encounters with Contemporary Art and Literature* (Cambridge and London: Harvard University Press, 1994).

6. *Minor Characters: A Young Woman's Coming of Age in the Beat Generation* (New York: Pocket Books, 1990). *How I Became Hettie Jones* (New York: Penguin, 1991).

7. Eve Kosofsky Sedgwick famously illuminates the political stakes of crossing identifications in *Epistemology of the Closet* (Berkeley and Los Angeles: University of California Press, 1990).

8. Carolyn G. Heilbrun makes the case in "Contemporary Memoirs, or, Who Cares Who Did What to Whom?" arguing against the diatribe published in *The Nation* cited in note 9, below. *The American Scholar* (summer 1999), 41.

9. Patrick Smith. "What Memoir Forgets," *The Nation* (July 27/August 3, 1998): 30.

10. Blaise Pascal, *Pensées*, in *Oeuvres complètes* (Paris: Gallimard, 1954), 1,126. Translation mine.

11. In "America, the Holocaust, and the Mass Culture of Memory: Toward a Radical Politics of Empathy," Alison Landsberg develops the notion of what she calls "prosthetic memories" to argue for an experiential model of approaching the memorialization of the Holocaust. Is it possible, she wonders, to produce a "bodily memory for those who have not lived through it"? *New German Critique* 71 (spring/summer 1997).

12. Shoshana Felman and Dori Laub, *Testimony: Crises of Witnessing in Literature, Psychoanalysis, and History* (New York and London: Routledge, 1992).

13. *Le Rouge et le Noir* (Paris: Garnier Flammarion, 1964) ch. 34, 442. Translation mine.

14. I've been slightly baffled to see Stendhal's novel crop up in just this way in Francine Prose's perverse *Blue Angel* (New York: HarperCollins, 2000), where the main character, a writer who has been trying to finish a novel called *The Black and the Black*, gets seduced (in part) by a student writer's passion for the original: "I love how Stendhal gets, you know, like, inside and outside Julien at the same time, so you can imagine doing what Julien's doing, and meanwhile you're thinking you would never do something like that" (38). Stendhal is also referenced in Philip Roth's *The Human Stain* as a way of trying to understand a piece of behavior as being . . . French (New York: Houghton Mifflin, 2000). Could the nineteenth-century realist novel be making a comeback?

15. *Recollections of My Life as a Woman: The New York Years* (New York: Viking, 2001).

16. Kerouac's line about the meaning of the Beat generation is quoted in *Burning Questions* (New York: Knopf, 1978), 47 Alix Kates Shulman's novel about New York life in the 1950s seen from a young woman's perspective.

17. In her autobiography, *Zami*, Lorde fictionalizes Burstein as Miss Burman, a teacher she had gone to see when she found herself pregnant. "She was one of the people I had consulted, and she wanted to have nothing to do with an abortion, saying I should have the baby. I didn't bother to tell her Black babies weren't adopted. They were absorbed into families, abandoned, or 'given up' " (111). But Burman comes to visit Audre in her Brighton Beach apartment. "Miss Burman, sympathetic but austere, stood quietly in the doorway, looking at my posters. . . . [She] lent me five dollars before she left" (112). *Zami: A New Spelling of My Name* (Trumansberg, N.Y.: Crossing Press, 1981).

2. DECADES

1. *Simone de Beauvoir* (New York and London: Virago/Pantheon, 1986), 13.

2. Marianne Hirsch and Evelyn Fox Keller, eds., *Conflicts in Feminism* (New York: Routledge, 1990).

3. I tried (unhappily) to address these issues in "Jason Dreams, Victoria Works Out," in *Generations: Feminisms in Dialogue*, Devoney Looser and E. Ann Kaplan, eds. (Minneapolis: University of Minnesota Press, 1997). But I was pleased to bring my students into the picture in their own words.

3. CIRCA 1959

1. Gayle Greene and Coppélia Kahn, eds., *Changing Subjects: The Making of Feminist Literary Criticism* (New York and London: Routledge, 1991).

2. Betty Friedan, *The Feminine Mystique* (1963; reprint, New York: Dell, 1984).

3. "The Other Night at Columbia: A Report from the Academy," in *Claremont Essays* (New York: Harcourt Brace, 1964).

4. *How I Became Hettie Jones* (New York: Penguin, 1991).

5. Catharine R. Stimpson. "Feminist Criticism," in *The Transformation of English and American Literary Studies*, Stephen Greenblatt and Giles Gunn, eds. (New York: MLA, 1992).

6. *Feminist Accused of Sexual Harassment* (Durham, N.C.: Duke University Press, 1997).

7. *Lettres à Nelson Algren: Un amour transatlantique. 1947–1964* (Paris: Gallimard, 1997). *A Transatlantic Love Affair* (New York: The New Press: 1998). In the French version there is no way of gauging Beauvoir's charm in these letters.

8. *Simone de Beauvoir: A Biography* (New York: Summit, 1990). Bair relied heavily on the letters to Algren in the biography, but they were not then available to the general public.

9. *Letters Home: Correspondence 1950–1963*, selected and edited with commentary by Aurelia Schober Plath (1975; reprint, New York: Harper Perennial, 1992).

10. *Promise of a Dream: Remembering the Sixties* (London: Penguin, 2001).

11. *Manhattan, When I Was Young* (New York: Houghton Mifflin, 1995).

12. *Sexual Politics* (New York: Doubleday, 1970).

13. *Flying* (1974; reprint, New York: Simon and Shuster, 1990).

14. "*Sexual Politics*: Twenty Years Later," *Women's Studies Quarterly* (1991): 3, 4. I'd like to thank Alix Kates Shulman for bringing this article to my attention.

15. The practice was named by Elaine Showalter in "Feminist Criticism in the Wilderness," in *The New Feminist Criticism: Essays on Women, Literature, Theory*, Elaine Showalter, ed. (New York: Pantheon, 1985).

16. I am beyond measure grateful to Judith Fryer Davidov for generously sharing with me her memories of this episode, as well as for her judicious editorial comments. And I would like to thank Tess Cosslett for inviting me to participate in the seminar "Autobiography and the Social Self," held by the Institute of Women's Studies at Lancaster University, which was where the writing of this chapter began.

4. THE MARKS OF TIME

1. The artist's description of the installation (ms.) explains that the supporting wooden base of the sculpture is integral to the conception of the autoportrait. The wood keeps working and develops cracks; the art, too, in this sense bears the marks of age and time. The installation, "A Collaborative Portfolio (Art, Photography, Poetry)," which was completed in 1992, was featured in *Feminist Studies* (summer 1995). The text includes a poem by Alicia Ostriker, "The Book of Life," and photographs by An-My Lê.

2. *An Accidental Autobiography* (Boston: Houghton, 1996).

3. "Alfred Chester's Wig," *New Yorker*, March 30, 1992, 79–98.

4. *Aging and Its Discontents: Freud and Other Fictions* (Bloomington: Indiana University Press, 1991). I wish to thank Kathleen Woodward for inviting me to the conference, "Women and Aging: Bodies, Cultures, Generations," which she organized at the Center for Twentieth Century Studies (1996) and that inspired me to begin work on this piece.

5. The passages in italics are excerpted from my *Bequest and Betrayal: Memoirs of a Parent's Death* (New York: Oxford, 1996; Bloomington: Indiana University Press, 2000).

6. *Elle* (November 1995): 158.

7. *The Education of a Woman: The Life of Gloria Steinem* (New York: Dial Press, 1995).

8. I have been unable to relocate this interview, but I know I haven't invented her words.

9. "Bodies of Knowledge," in *Revolution from Within: A Book of Self-Esteem* (Boston, Toronto, London: Little, Brown, 1992).

10. *Of Woman Born* (New York: Norton, 1976).

11. Mira Schor, interview with Stuart Horodner in the catalogue for the exhibition at the Horodner Gallery, New York, N.Y., October 5–November 6, 1993, n.p.

12. *Cultural Sniping: The Art of Transgression* (London and New York: Routledge, 1995).

13. *The Autobiography of a Face* (Boston: Houghton, 1994).

14. *A Celebration of One Hundred Years: The New York Times Magazine*, April 14, 1996.

15. Susan Sachs, *New York Times*, March 28, 1999.

16. *Exteriors*, trans. Tanya Leslie (New York: Seven Stories Press, 1996).

17. *Simone de Beauvoir: A Biography* (New York: Summit Books, 1990).

18. *The Autobiography of Simone de Beauvoir: Hard Times: Force of Circumstance II*, trans. Richard Howard, with an introduction by Toril Moi (1963; reprint, New York: Paragon House, 1992).

19. *All Said and Done*, trans. Patrick O'Brien (1974; reprint, New York: Warner Books, 1976).

20. *The Lover*, trans. Barbara Bray (1985; reprint, New York: Perennial, 1986). Bethany Ladimer's *Colette, Beauvoir, and Duras: Age and Women Writers* (Gainesville: University Press of Florida, 1999) provides an illuminating study of the ways in which French women writers have dealt with aging.

21. *Moving Beyond Words* (New York: Simon and Shuster, 1994).

22. Julie Burchill, Column, "Vanities," *Vanity Fair* (June 1994): 86, 88.

23. *The Last Gift of Time* (New York: Dial Press, 1997).

24. *Times* (London), August 12, 2001, 4. I have been unable to locate the agency that had the rights to that picture. The photograph I reproduce here, however, comes from the series of photos that included the one that appeared in the *Times*—same haircomb, earrings, top, and so on. Oddly, the photos are dated 1995—the same year as the interviews from which I have been quoting, when Deneuve was fifty-one not fifty-seven.

5. "WHY AM I NOT THAT WOMAN?"

1. *Exteriors*, trans. Tanya Leslie (New York: Seven Stories Press, 1996), 41, TM. The abbreviation TM indicates that the published translation has been modified by me.

2. *Rousseau, Judge of Jean-Jacques: Dialogues*, ed. Roger D. Masters and Christopher Kelley, trans. Judith R. Bush, Christopher Kelley, and Roger D. Masters (Hanover: University Press of New England, 1990), 118.

3. Ernaux receives a voluminous correspondence from readers who often feel she has told their story. In her excellent study *Annie Ernaux: An Introduction to the Writer and Her Audience* (Oxford: Berg, 1999), Lyn Thomas analyzes this phenomenon along with other instances of identification that Ernaux's work produces in her readers.

4. *A Woman's Story*, trans. Tanya Leslie (New York: Four Walls Eight Windows, 1991).

5. *A Man's Place*, trans. Tanya Leslie (New York: Four Walls Eight Windows, 1992), 13, TM.

6. *La Vie extérieure: 1993–1999* (Paris: Gallimard, 2000).

7. *Shame*, trans. Tanya Leslie (New York: Seven Stories Press, 1998).

8. *Moments of Being*, ed. Jeanne Schulkind (New York: HBJ, 1985).

9. *Emile*, book 1, 249 in the Pléiade edition, quoted in *Rousseau* (above 265).

10. In transcribing the quotation from Rousseau, Ernaux moves the emphasis from the noun *self* to the adjective *true*, "notre vrai *moi*." *Rousseau Juge de Jean-Jacques: Deuxième dialogue, oeuvres complètes*, vol. 1, Bernard Gangebin and Marcel Raymond, eds. (Paris: Gallimard, 1959). I thank Dennis Hollier for inviting me to "One Hundred Years of Egos and Others" (October 1993) at Yale University, where I presented the first part of this chapter. And

Michael Riffaterre for his insights about autobiography's others. (Dartmouth College, June 1988.)

EPILOGUE

1. *Unfinished People: Eastern European Jews Encounter America* (New York and London: Norton, 1996), 147.

2. Joyce Mendelsohn, *Lower East Side: Remembered and Revisited* (New York: The Lower East Side Press, 2001), 101.

3. Salo W. Baron. *The Russian Jew Under Tsars and Soviets* (New York: Schocken, 1987), 57.

4. *Roland Barthes by Roland Barthes*, trans. Richard Howard (New York: Farrar, Straus and Giroux, 1989).

5. *Patrimony: A True Story* (New York: Simon and Schuster, 1991), 238.